# Collins
## revision guides

CW00340276

**Active**Revision

# GCSEEnglish

Pam Bloomfield

Series editor: Jayne de Courcy

Published by HarperCollins*Publishers* Ltd
77-85 Fulham Palace Road
London W6 8JB

www.collinseducation.com
On-line support for schools and colleges

© HarperCollins*Publishers* Ltd 2004

First published 2004
10 9 8 7 6 5 4 3 2 1

ISBN 0 00 717542 6 (with CD)
ISBN 0 00 718503 0

Pam Bloomfield asserts the moral right to be identified as the author of this work.

**British Library Cataloguing in Publication Data**
A catalogue record for this book is available from the British Library.

Edited by Nancy Candlin
Series and book design by Sally Boothroyd
Illustrations by Virginia Gray and Anthony Maher
Index compiled by Julie Rimington
Production by Katie Butler
Printed and bound by Printing Express, Hong Kong

The enclosed CD-ROM will run on **PC** and **Macintosh** computers that meet (or exceed) the following specifications:

**For PCs:** Intel Pentium III 550 MHz (or equivalent) processor, Microsoft® Windows 98SE/Me/2000/XP, 64Mb RAM, 16-bit color monitor capable of 1024x768 resolution, CD-ROM drive.

**For Macintosh:** Power PC, MacOS 9.1, 64Mb RAM, 16-bit color monitor capable of 1024x768 resolution; CD-ROM drive.

# CONTENTS

# ABOUT THIS BOOK AND CD-ROM

## HOW THIS BOOK WILL HELP YOU

**ActiveRevision GCSE English** is an entirely new way to revise and boost your GCSE grade. The book and CD-ROM work **interactively** to help you assess your strengths, target your weaknesses and polish your skills.

**ActiveRevision GCSE English** will help you to prepare for your exam by:

- revising key reading and writing skills (**Book**)
- testing you on these skills (**CD-ROM**)
- helping you to approach exam questions with confidence (**Book and CD-ROM**)
- helping you to plan your revision time effectively (**CD-ROM**).

## WHAT THE BOOK CONTAINS

### Reading

This section is divided into **non-fiction/media**, **fiction** and **poetry**. There are lots of examples of the different types of texts and questions you will meet in your exam. You are shown how to analyse texts closely through **annotation**, and **how to plan and write responses** to questions. All of this will help you to achieve a C grade or better in your Reading questions in your GCSE exam.

### Writing

This section focuses on the **different types of writing** you may need to produce in your exam, such as writing to persuade, writing to argue or writing to inform. You are given the chance to revise the specific requirements of each type of writing. Examples of **good quality exam responses** demonstrate what is needed and will boost your confidence. All of this will help you to achieve a C grade or better in your Writing task in your GCSE exam.

### Exam practice

This section gives you examples of GCSE Reading and Writing questions that you can try answering. **Sample answers** at C grade and above are given at the back of the Book, for you to compare with your own answers. There is **clear guidance** on how examiners assess answers to each type of question so that **you know exactly what you need to do** to achieve a C grade or better.

## HOW TO MAKE THE BEST USE OF THIS BOOK AND CD–ROM

Everyone has their own strengths and weaknesses, so the way in which you use **ActiveRevision GCSE English** is up to you. The **contents list** provides a good starting point and you can then decide which of the following approaches suits you better:

### Option 1 – Work steadily through the Book and CD-ROM

1. Obtain a copy of your GCSE exam specification from your teacher. Then, on the **contents list** at the start of this Book, tick off all the Reading and Writing units you need to cover.

2. One by one, read through each unit in the Book and do the accompanying test on the CD-ROM.

3. If you don't score high marks on a test, tick the **'revise again'** column in the contents list, which will help you keep track of which areas you need to spend more time on.

4. If you do score high marks on a test, tick the **'revised and understood'** column in the contents list.

5. Once you have done most of the tests, the **Revision Planner** on the CD-ROM will help you to prioritise the areas on which you need to spend further revision time.

### Option 2 – Concentrate on your weak areas first

If you are short of time, you could opt for a more selective approach to your English revision. In this case you could:

1. Obtain a copy of your GCSE exam specification from your teacher. Then, on the **contents list** at the start of this Book, tick off all the Reading and Writing units you need to cover.

2. Decide which areas you think are your weakest and try the tests on the CD-ROM.

3. If you don't score high marks on these tests, read through the units in the Book and then try the tests again.

4. If you have time, try the tests for some of the areas about which you feel confident, just to check you're not being over-confident!

5. Once you have done most of these tests, the **Revision Planner** on the CD-ROM will help you to prioritise the areas on which you need to spend further revision time.

Remember, whichever option you choose, use the Book and CD-ROM interactively to give instant feedback on your strengths and weaknesses.

# HOW TO INSTALL YOUR CD-ROM

To run the Active Revision application, you just need to double-click on the file called `ar.exe` (or `ar.hqx` if you're using a Mac) on the CD-ROM. On some computers it will start automatically when you put the disc into the CD-ROM drive.

For minimum specifications to run the CD-ROM, see page 2.

If the application then appears in a small window, you can hold down the CTRL key and press F to make it fill the whole screen.

## 1. WELCOME SCREEN

This is the first screen that you will see. Once the data has finished loading, click on the **"Continue"** button to get to the Main Menu.

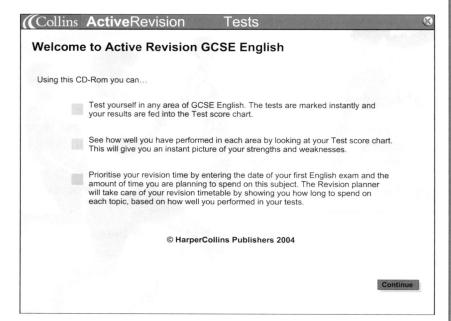

## 2. MAIN MENU

You can select tests in four areas: Reading Non-fiction, **Reading Fiction**, Reading Poetry and Writing. Just click on the one you want to do.

Alternatively, click on one of the buttons at the bottom of the screen and this will take you to your **Test Score Chart**, the **Poetry Revision Charts** or the **Revision Planner** (see page 9).

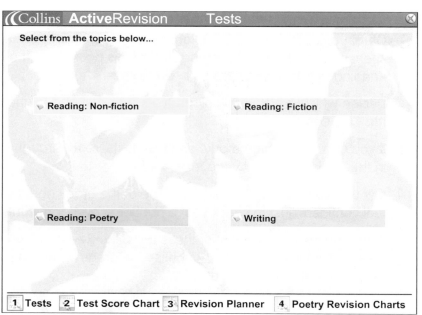

## 3. THE TESTS

**Selecting the test you want**
Once you are in your selected test area, click on the test you want.

**Carrying out the tests**
There are over 20 tests altogether, linked to the units in the book. Each test tells you exactly what you have to do – and gives you invaluable practice in the skills you need for your exam.

If you need help before starting a test, click on the **"Help" button**. Click on it again and the Help text will disappear.

With most of the tests, you can change your mind and alter things as you are completing the test. However, with some tests this is not possible and you will need to click on the **"Restart Question" button**. Where this is necessary, it is clearly stated in the **"What to do" box**.

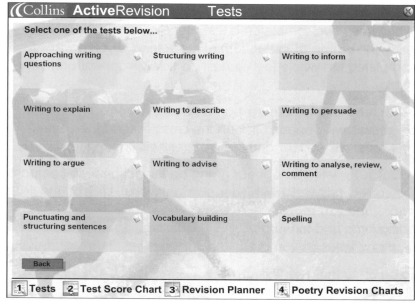

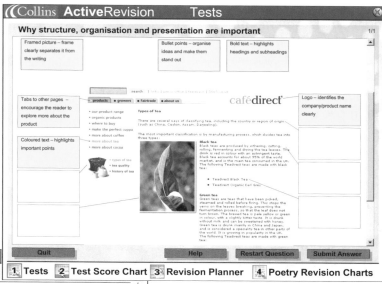

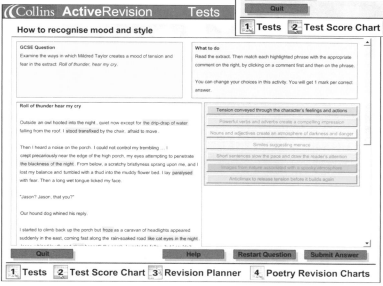

## Instant feedback

When you have completed a test, just click on the "Submit Answer" button at the bottom of the screen. If you have completed the whole test correctly, a tick will appear and your marks.

If you have completed any part of the test incorrectly, a cross or crosses will appear. Click on the cross(es) and the correct answer(s) will appear and the cross(es) will change to tick(s).

A Quick Tip will also appear giving additional help. To compare the correct answer(s) with your own answer(s), click on the tick(s) again. You can move backwards and forwards as many times as you like.

To go on to the next test, click the "Next >" button. Or, if you want to return to the test selection menu, click on the "Quit" button. (Note: you must click on the Quick Tip box so that it disappears before you can move on.)

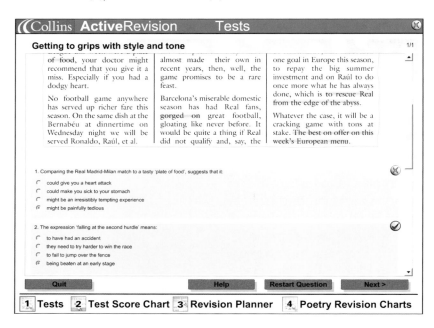

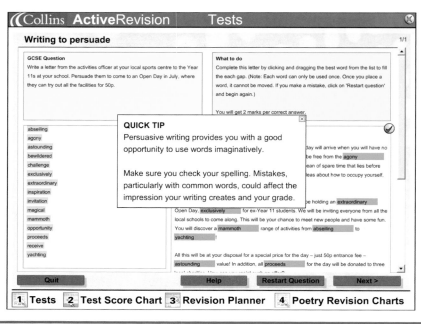

## 4. TEST SCORE CHART

Once you have completed a test, your marks are fed into the **Test Score Chart** so that you have **a record of which tests you have completed and how well you have done**. Your results are colour coded so you can see at a glance your strengths and weaknesses. Remember, if you feel it will help, **you can redo a test** – perhaps after going back over the relevant unit in the book. The **Test Score Chart** will keep a record of **your latest score only**.

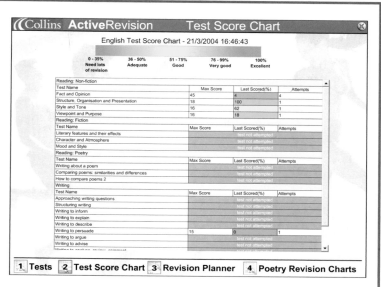

## 5. REVISION PLANNER

Once you have completed most of the tests, the **Revision Planner** will help you to **prioritise your remaining English revision time**. All you have to do is enter the date of your first English exam, and how many hours you want to revise English per week. You will then be shown the areas on which it might be best for you to spend your remaining revision time – based on how you have performed in the tests. The **Revision Planner changes as you complete or redo tests**, and as you get nearer to the exam.

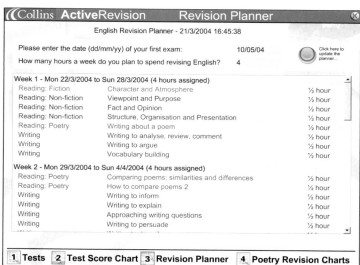

## 6. POETRY REVISION CHARTS

**Revision Chart 1** allows you to **create a chart for each poem that you are revising**. You can enter your own notes under the headings given or change the headings. **Revision Chart 2** automatically takes the names of the poems from Chart 1 and **allows you to compare them** by putting ticks under thematic headings. (Again, you can change these headings to suit your poems.)

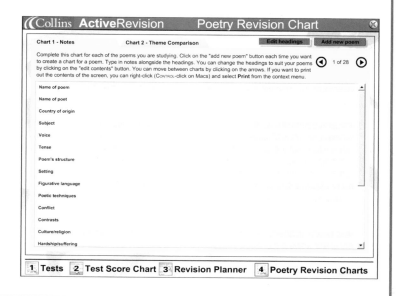

# HOW TO TELL FACT FROM OPINION

- You need to be able to tell the difference between fact and opinion.

- You need to understand how the writer's selection and presentation of facts can influence the reader.

- You must be able to comment on the way in which opinions communicate the writer's point of view.

This is a GCSE-style question (or part of a question):

**Comment on how the writer uses facts and opinions to produce an effect on the reader.** Support your answer with examples from the text.

KEY  CONCEPTS

Fact: **something that is known to be true and can be proved to be so, e.g.** Giraffes have the longest necks of all animals – **this could be verified.**

Opinion: **something that is a belief or judgment, which others may agree or disagree with, according to their point of view, e.g.** Giraffes are beautiful and graceful creatures – **what is beautiful and graceful to one person may not be to another.**

## THINKING ABOUT FACTS AND OPINIONS

When reading the text, consider the following:

### 1. How to begin

Highlight facts in one colour (e.g. yellow).
Highlight opinions in another colour (e.g. green).

This will help you to:
- be clear about what is fact and what is opinion
- understand the balance between fact and opinion
- identify examples for use later on.

### 2. Next, examine the way in which the writer has selected and used the facts.

For example:
- Do the facts represent just **one point of view**?
- Is there a **balance** between positive and negative facts?
- Do you feel that some facts may have been deliberately omitted?

### 3. Then look at how opinions have been stated.

- Are some of the opinions presented as if they are facts?
- Do you feel that the writer has used opinions to **persuade** or **influence** the reader?
- Is there a link between the facts and the opinions in terms of the overall **point of view** of the text?

### 4. Finally, think about the overall impact of the facts and opinions on the reader.

Do they:
- give the reader a balanced or one-sided point of view?
- try to persuade or influence the reader?
- give the reader **the writer's personal perspective** or a broader, **impersonal perspective**?

## HOW TO ANNOTATE A TEXT

The suggestions on the previous page can be used to analyse the text and prepare an answer to the exam question.

# Small is beautiful: the Maldives are an island paradise

**Mark Carwardine**

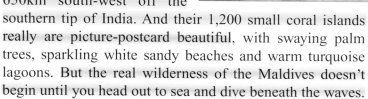

**Key**

Opinions

Facts

*Straightforward fact*

*An opinion that is presented as a fact*

Why choose the Maldives for my favourite wilderness destination? Well, they're certainly remote, splashed across the Indian Ocean some 650km south-west off the southern tip of India. And their 1,200 small coral islands really are picture-postcard beautiful, with swaying palm trees, sparkling white sandy beaches and warm turquoise lagoons. But the real wilderness of the Maldives doesn't begin until you head out to sea and dive beneath the waves.

*Positive fact – have negative facts been omitted here?*

*Negative fact of the area being crowded is turned into a positive opinion*

*Positive opinion expressed in unbeatable terms*

The Maldives is so beautiful under water that, at first, it is difficult to know where to look. The reefs are teeming with life and, so far, more than 1,100 species of fish and 250 corals have been recorded around the archipelago. The water temperature is like a warm bath and, especially towards the end of the north-east monsoon in March and April, the visibility can be outstanding. On some occasions, it is possible to see a breathtaking 70 metres down the coral edge towards the seabed. And with just a little effort, it's possible to get away from the crowds and enjoy one of the world's most impressive underwater wildernesses in relative peace and quiet.

The Maldives is also one of the best places in the tropics – perhaps even the world – for whale- and dolphin-watching, and yet, strangely, it seems to have gone largely unnoticed, and so it's possible to sail for hours – or even days – without seeing another soul.

*Negative fact that the nights are long is turned into a positive*

*Opinion designed to persuade the reader*

Finally, one of the great measures of real wilderness is complete and utter darkness. In the Maldives, it is dark for about 12 hours every day of the year, and if you're on a boat miles from the nearest inhabited island, you can watch the stars multiply into hundreds or even thousands. They seem much brighter here, too. Sometimes the entire sky is alive with shooting stars, and then there's nothing better than lying on the deck, staring into space.

## HOW TO PLAN YOUR ANSWER

- Even in your exam, where you are working against the clock, it is important to spend time looking at the text in detail and to think about your response.

- You need to use questions like those on page 10 to structure your answer and to gather examples and quotations to support the points you make. Plan your answer in note form to save time.

---

- **What is the balance between fact and opinion?**

  *Fairly balanced. A few more opinions than facts.*

- **Do the facts represent just one point of view?**

  *Yes – mostly present a positive image of the islands, e.g. 'with swaying palm trees' and 'it's possible to sail for hours – or even days – without seeing another soul.'*

- **Is there a balance between negative and positive facts?**

  *No – very few negative facts – just one reference to 'crowds' and the hours of darkness.*

- **Do you feel that some facts may have been deliberately omitted?**

  *Yes – very little said about crowds/the cost/how long it takes to get there.*

- **Are some of the opinions presented as if they are facts?**

  *Yes – 'really are picture-postcard beautiful' sounds like a fact, but what seems good to one person may not be to another.*

- **Do you feel that the writer has used opinions to persuade or influence the reader?**

  *Yes – many of the opinions use words of great praise, e.g. 'the world's most impressive' and 'one of the best places'.*

- **Is there a link between the facts and the opinions in terms of the overall point of view of the text?**

  *Yes – facts and opinions are combined to give a positive, personal point of view, e.g. 'it is possible to see a breathtaking 70 metres down the coral edge towards the seabed' – '70 metres' is a fact but 'breathtaking' is an opinion.*

- **What impact does the presentation of facts and opinions have on the reader?**

  *A one-sided point of view. The aim is to persuade the reader that the Maldives is a perfect holiday destination. At the end it says 'you can watch the stars multiply into hundreds...there's nothing better than lying on the deck, staring into space.' First part is fact; second part is opinion. Reader is caught up in the mixture of fact and opinion – easy to mistake opinion for fact.*

## HOW TO WRITE YOUR ANSWER

**Remember to:**
- keep to the point of the task set
- ensure that all your comments and examples are relevant.

The text has a fairly even mix of facts and opinions. Facts such as the 'swaying palm trees' and 'the reefs are teeming with life' give a very positive picture of the islands. The writer only includes two negative facts: the first is a quick mention of 'crowds', which is not fully explained. The second is when he says that 'it is dark for about 12 hours every day of the year' but then goes on to express his opinion that this is a good thing because you can watch the stars for hours. Because the writer does not say anything about the cost or how long it takes to get there, the reader may not realise that there are drawbacks to this 'paradise'.

Another technique that the writer uses to make an impression on the reader is to offer opinions as facts. He says that the coral islands 'really are picture-postcard beautiful', which sounds like a fact but is really an opinion, because what looks good to one person may not to another. The author also tends to give his opinion by using words of very high praise, such as 'the world's most impressive' or 'one of the best places', which are bound to influence the reader.

Facts and opinions are sometimes joined together, supporting the positive picture of the islands that the author is presenting. It is sometimes difficult to tell them apart. For example, the writer says: 'it is possible to see abreathtaking 70 metres down the coral edge towards the seabed'. 'Breathtaking' is an opinion, not a fact, but a lot of readers might not realise this.

Overall the writer uses positive facts and his own personal opinions to present a biased point of view in order to convince the reader that the Maldives is a perfect holiday destination for people who love nature. One further example that supports this is at the end of the passage where it says 'you can watch the stars multiply into hundreds...there's nothing better than lying on the deck, staring into space.' This is a clever mixture of fact and opinion that sets out to persuade the reader that the Maldives are a great place to go for a 'wilderness' experience.

### Why this is a good response

This answer:
- makes the difference between fact and an opinion clear
- demonstrates how both facts and opinions can influence the reader
- discusses ways in which facts and opinions have been used to persuade the reader
- uses relevant examples from the text to support comments made.

To test yourself, go to Reading: Non-fiction – Fact and opinion.

# WHY STRUCTURE, ORGANISATION AND PRESENTATION ARE IMPORTANT

- In your exam, you may be asked to comment on three important elements of a media (or other non-fiction) text: structure, organisation and presentation.

- You are likely to be asked how these influence the reader's understanding.

This is a GCSE-style question (or part of a question):

**Examine the ways in which the article *Pay as you learn* conveys information about the programme it is promoting. You should comment on:**
- **structure**
- **organisation**
- **presentation.**
Support your answer with examples from the text.

## KEY 🔑 CONCEPTS

> **Structure:** the way in which the writer uses devices such as paragraphs, headings and punctuation to make the content clear and easily understood.
>
> **Organisation:** the way in which the content is ordered to gain the reader's interest and understanding.
>
> **Presentation:** the way in which a text is laid out on the page or on-screen.

## THINKING ABOUT STRUCTURE, ORGANISATION AND PRESENTATION

### How to begin

The key words in the question – **structure, organisation, and presentation** – indicate that the focus of your answer must be on these features, rather than on the content or persuasive language of the article.

These are the main features that you should look out for in the text:

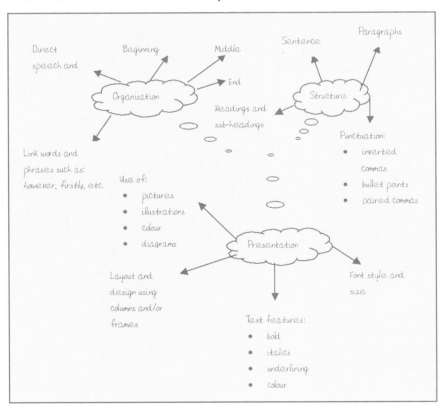

## HOW TO ANALYSE A TEXT

The extract below has been annotated. Words and phrases that relate to the writer's tone and style have been highlighted, so that these may be built into the response later.

*Can schools like this make a difference?*

*Title of TV programme – smaller font size*

**A Second Chance Sundays C4**

# Pay as you learn

*Main heading:*
- *large font*
- *play on words earn/learn*

*A major new experiment puts private schools under the microscope*

*Quotation*

At the start of the documentary series *A Second Chance*, 14-year-old Ryan Bell is described by teachers at his south London comprehensive as "rude and unmanageable". But after a year at £15,000-a-year Downside School in Somerset, he's top in two subjects and star of the rugby team.

*Sub-heading – draws the reader into the text*

*Italics used to distinguish the tile of the TV programme*

*Interview clip – quotation*

*Direct speech*

"He's part of the family," beams headmaster Dom Antony Sutch. "I'm proud of him, he's proud of himself," smiles Ryan's mum, Jacqui. But what does Ryan's story tell us? "First, I think it shows we give up on our teenagers too easily," says executive producer Trevor Phillips, whose TV company, Pepper Productions, will pay Ryan's fees for the next three years.

*Question – answered later in the article*

*Indicates introduction of the first point*

*Indicates introduction of the second point*

"Second, it shows that class size is important – at Ryan's old school, the teachers just weren't able to cope with all his questions. At Downside (average class size 16), they can give him more time."

*Round brackets indicate additional information*

Phillips, who made the series before being appointed chairman for the Commission for Racial Equality, doesn't believe it's all down to money, either. "Strip away the food and accommodation costs, and parents are probably paying £5,000 – £6,000 [a year] to send their children to Downside. The State spends around £4,000 – £5,000 per pupil. It's not that public schools spend more money – they stretch its effects much further."

*Paired commas include/indicate additional material*

*Square brackets clarify information*

However, the series is not all happy-ever-after stories. One of the two other *A Second Chance* "experiments" fizzles out when the girl decides to leave her new school. "For some kids, the gap between the reality of home life and the expectations of school just can't be bridged," reflects Phillips.

And even Ryan had his ups and downs – he was suspended for two weeks after a "prank" involving someone else's mobile phone. But he's back at school now, and more determined than ever to succeed.

*Christopher Middleton*

*Link word introducing another side of the argument*

*Dash used to introduce a 'by the way' comment*

*Inverted commas suggest the word is being used in an offbeat way*

*Columns help to break up the text*

## HOW TO PLAN YOUR ANSWER

- Pick out examples from your analysis of the text.
- Plan your responses briefly in a logical order.

### Structure

#### Headings
- The title of the programme is in a small font; the title of the article is in a large font and different style; the sub-heading is in italics.

#### Paragraphs and sentences
- A variety of punctuation is needed to make the long sentences clear.
- Inverted commas around phrases used in a slightly unusual way, e.g. "experiments", as well as around spoken words and quotations from interviews.
- Paired commas: Phillips, who made the series before... Racial Equality,
- Brackets: (average class size 16)
- Single dash: – at Ryan's old school

### Organisation

#### Beginning
- Summary of what the programme will cover.

#### Middle
- Explores what the programme reveals about the relationship between teenagers and their schools.

#### End
- Puts a different, more negative side, but ends on a high note.

#### Devices – link words and direct speech/quotation
- The question 'But what does Ryan's story tell us?' introduces an explanation.
- 'At the start', 'First', 'Second' and 'However' provide links between paragraphs.
- Interview clips include "I'm proud of him".
- There is a direct quotation: "rude and unmanageable".

### Presentation

#### Layout and design
- Different sizes and styles of font used for headings and main text.
- Change from one column at the start to two later on helps to break up the text.

#### Textual presentation features
- Italics used to pick out the title of the TV programme, heading in bold.

#### Visual props
- Picture creates interest.

Why structure, organisation and presentation are important!

## HOW TO WRITE YOUR ANSWER

**Remember to:**
- focus on the areas emphasised in the bullet points of the exam question
- organise your comments logically according to topic (structure/organisation/presentation), rather than in the order they occur in the text
- avoid becoming too involved in the content.

---

The article 'Pay as you learn', a review about a television programme 'A Second Chance', uses organisation, structure and presentation to attract the attention of the reader and help their understanding.

The writer has organised the piece by beginning with a brief summary of what the programme is about, followed by a discussion of some of the issues that it tackles. He closes his piece by bringing in a negative element before finishing on a positive note. Within the text, links such as 'At the start', 'First', 'Second' and 'However' are used as prompts that give the reader direction; as well as a question, 'But what does Ryan's story tell us?', which is then answered. There are also quotations, e.g. "rude and unmanageable", and interview clips, e.g. "I'm proud of him", which help to make the story seem more real to the reader.

Headings are used to structure the article only at the start. Paragraphs of similar lengths are used to introduce different topics and break up the content. The writer uses complex sentences that become quite long when extra information is given. Different types of punctuation are used to help make the long sentences clear. For example, the author uses paired commas: 'Phillips, who made the series before...Racial Equality,'; brackets: '(average class size 16)'; and a single dash: '- at Ryan's old school'. Inverted commas are used to mark quotations from interviews, e.g. "He's part of the family," as well as around phrases that have been used in a slightly unusual way, e.g. "experiments" and "prank".

The presentation of the article, in particular the layout and design, helps to break up the text and make it look interesting. For example, different sizes and styles of fonts are used for the headings: the title of the programme is in small type; the title of the article itself is in a large, bold font; underneath is an explanation of the article in italics. The main text then changes from one column at the start to two later on, which also adds interest. The use of a photograph draws the reader into the article.

### Why this is a good response

*Introduction shows a clear understanding of the task*

*Brief outline of the content linked with organisation only*

*Fine detail supported by examples from the text*

*A number of points being made here, some of which are supported by examples from the text*

*The main points are covered here, but there is a 'rushed' feel and the response lacks a conclusion*

*Overall, this is a well-organised response*

---

To test yourself, go to Reading: Non-fiction – Structure, organisation and presentation.

# GETTING TO GRIPS WITH STYLE AND TONE

- You need to be able to explain how different styles of writing attract readers.

- You need to appreciate the way in which the tone of the writing influences the reader's understanding of what is being said.

- You need to recognise the devices writers use, understand how they work and comment on the effect they create.

This is a GCSE-style question (or part of a question)

**How does the writer's tone and style engage the interest of the reader?**
Support your answer with examples from the text.

## THINKING ABOUT STYLE AND TONE

**How to begin**
When reading the text, ask yourself three main questions:

**1. Is the text written from a personal or impersonal point of view?**

Look to see whether is it:
- written from a personal perspective – using the first person (**I, my, we, us, ours**) or sometimes the second person (**you, yours**)
- written from an impersonal point of view – using the third person (**she/he/it, his/hers, they/theirs**).

**2. Has the writer used a formal or informal tone?**

Look at the language and expression and decide whether it is:
- formal and serious, perhaps using some technical words or complex sentence structures
- informal and light-hearted, perhaps using casual or slang expressions, with a hint of humour.

KEY 🔑 CONCEPTS

Tone: **the attitude and atmosphere that is communicated to the reader, created by the writer's vocabulary and sentence structure.**

Style: **the method and approaches that a writer uses, for example through an imaginative choice of words, and use of literary devices such as figurative language.**

**3. How has the writer engaged the interest of the reader?**

Use this checklist as a guide of things to look out for:
- powerful/unusual verbs – such as **scuttle, plummet, elude**
- interesting adjectives – for example **azure** rather than simply **blue**
- figurative language – such as similes, metaphors, personification
- word sounds – for example alliteration, onomatopoeia
- clichés – over-used words and phrases such as **basically, to be honest**
- slang expressions – an indicator of informality, for example. **kids, 'cos, batty**
- variety of sentence construction and length
- direct speech or a quotation – often brings the writing alive
- humour – not necessarily something that makes you laugh out loud.

## HOW TO ANNOTATE A TEXT

The extract below has been annotated.
Words and phrases that relate to the writer's
tone and style have been highlighted, so that
these may later be built into the response.

# Thoughts of a Golden Girl

### Tanni Grey-Thompson

*Born with spina bifida and unable to use her legs, Tanni, now a famous athlete, reflects on experiences that are part of her remarkable life.*

*Informal language* — *Signalling the start of a narrative* — *Interesting adjective*

*Personal point of view (perspective)* — *Humorous imagery – including a simile and alliteration (flapping, floor, fish)* — *Powerful verbs*

Kids are just very blunt and inquiring, whereas adults sometimes make things worse by trying too hard to treat you normally. Once, I fell out of my chair while rushing to get somewhere in Birmingham. I was carrying a stack of paper and wasn't looking where I was going. I fell into a puddle of mushy leaves and the contents of my bag went flying. There I was, flapping around on the floor like a dying fish, when I noticed a man looking at me. It was as if it was an everyday experience to see a person sprawled on the floor like that. Then he must have realised who I was because he came over to me.

*Direct speech*

"You're Tanni Grey," he said.

*Formal language*

"That's right," I said trying to hide my embarrassment. And he proceeded to talk to me in depth about the Paralympics and the London Marathon and Birmingham hosting the World Championships. I was nodding and scrambling around like an idiot, picking up two pence pieces as he carried on.

*Figurative language – simile*

*Variation in sentence length*

Then he said, "Right, I'd better be off," and he left me there, lying on the floor in a puddle. It was odd, but I think it was probably down to the fact that he didn't know what to do. People are like that a lot. They don't know how to react around disabled people and feel embarrassed…

*Reflection – speaking directly to the reader*

That's all part of what it's like to be disabled. But the truth is I do not have the typical life of a disabled person.

## HOW TO PLAN YOUR RESPONSE

- The questions on page 18 will help you to find the information that is needed to answer the question well.

- The points made need to be supported by evidence (usually a quotation) and a comment.

### 1. Is the text written from a personal or impersonal point of view?

(Deal with this first as it is usually quite straightforward.)

**Point**

A personal point of view.

**Evidence** (Give an example, usually a quotation or reference to the text.)

'I fell out of my chair'

**Comment** (Is this approach suitable for the purpose? How does it affect you as a reader?)

Suitable – as a reader I feel as if the writer is speaking to me directly, telling her story.

### 2. Has the writer used a formal or informal tone?

(This helps you to move into an area where greater discussion is needed.)

**Point**

Informal and formal styles of writing are used – matching the language with the content.

**Evidence** (Give an example, usually a quotation or reference to the text.)

At the beginning, Tanni uses an informal expression, 'Kids are just very blunt', but later her style is more formal when she says, 'he proceeded to talk to me in depth'.

**Comment** (Is this style appropriate for the purpose?)

This mixture of styles helps to make the writing interesting and holds the reader's attention as it is not all the same.

### 3. How has the writer's style engaged the interest of the reader?

(This should form the main body of your answer – make several points here, supported by examples.)

- powerful verbs e.g. 'scrambling'

- interesting adjectives e.g. 'mushy'

- direct speech e.g. 'You're Tanni Grey'

- figurative language e.g. 'like an idiot'

- humorous imagery e.g. 'flapping around on the floor like a dying fish'

- mainly long sentences but one powerful short one in last paragraph.

## HOW TO WRITE YOUR ANSWER

**Remember to:**
- address the question directly
- follow the 'point, evidence, comment' guidelines
- use inverted commas to show where there are quotations
- avoid using a quotation more than once
- select key points.

One of the main ways in which the writer has engaged the reader's interest is by writing from a personal point of view, for example 'I fell out of my chair'. This approach helps me, the reader, to feel as if the writer is speaking to me directly as she tells her story.

Secondly, the reader's interest is caught by the way the writer uses both informal and formal tones to match her language to what she wants to say. For example, at the beginning she uses an informal expression, 'Kids are just very blunt'; later on, her style is more formal when she says, 'he proceeded to talk to me in depth'. This mixture of styles helps to vary the writing, make it more interesting and hold the attention of the reader.

Finally, the author has used a number of different elements of style to make her writing interesting and entertaining. There are, for example, powerful verbs such as 'scrambling' and 'sprawled', which attract my attention. 'Mushy' is an interesting adjective to describe the fallen leaves and she also uses two strong similes, 'like an idiot' and 'flapping around on the floor like a dying fish'. This second simile makes use of alliteration and creates a powerful, funny image, which adds to the informal tone. Many of the sentences are quite long but she introduces a short one in the last paragraph: 'People are like that a lot'; this makes this sentence more powerful and memorable. Introducing direct speech, starting with 'You're Tanni Grey', helps to break up what would otherwise be a straightforward account and makes it more realistic and interesting.

**Why this is a good response**
This answer:
- addresses the question directly
- keeps to the point at all times
- uses examples and comments to support points made
- is clearly structured using three paragraphs
- shows an understanding of how tone and style work to create interest for the reader.

To test yourself, go to Reading: Non-fiction – Style and tone.

# UNDERSTANDING VIEWPOINT AND PURPOSE

- You need to understand why a text has been written – that is, its purpose.

- You must be able to follow an argument or point of view.

- You need to be able to comment on the ways in which the language of a text creates an effect.

Some GCSE questions may ask you to consider different aspects of a text through a series of shorter questions:

**Read the article from *BBC Wildlife* by Jonathon Porritt on page 23.**

**You are being asked to follow an argument and select material appropriate to its purpose.**

1. Explain, in your own words, why 'Remote, beautiful and pristine places such as Antarctica' may, in the writer's opinion, one day 'be wildernesses no longer'. *(4 marks)*

**You are now being asked to focus on the language of the article.**

2. Examine how the writer's expression affects the reader. *(6 marks)*

**You are now being asked to focus on the purpose of the article.**

3. What do you consider the writer's intentions and objectives to be? *(5 marks)*

KEY 🔑 CONCEPTS

> Purpose: **the function and intention of the writing.**
>
> Viewpoint: **an attitude or point of view.**

## THINKING ABOUT VIEWPOINT AND PURPOSE

**How to begin**

- **Annotate** the text, picking out evidence and the main points that will help you to answer the questions.
- Use different-coloured highlighters or use the numbering of the question to **distinguish** which information helps you with which answer.
- Choose only the best examples to support your responses.

**Remember!**

In answers to short questions like these you need to:
- get to the point quickly
- use quotations as evidence to support your points
- avoid repeating the same quotation in your answers to different parts of the question
- make sure that you don't give information in an earlier answer that is more necessary in a later one.

## HOW TO ANNOTATE A TEXT

**Key**

Focus on question 1

Focus on question 2

Focus on question 3

*Words that appeal to the emotions (emotive terms)*

*Casual, chatty tone, as if he's talking to us*

*Ironic tone*

*Persuasive argument*

*Target reader (us and them)*

*Cliché making the reader agree with the point that follows*

*Belittles their argument by insulting them*

*Sounds like a warning*

*Information*

*Introduces argument*

*Central arguments*

*Central point*

*Slang expression makes him one of us*

*Persuasion*

*Central point*

*Persuasive point*

# Jonathon Porritt

**Remote, beautiful and pristine places such as Antarctica are having to 'work' increasingly hard to justify their wilderness status – so that one day they may be wildernesses no longer.**

So now they're going to build a road to the South Pole – all the way from the place where the tourists disembark to the very heart of the continent. To support scientific work, it's said. But how long before Antarctica's growing tourism business gets a look in? To me, this demonstrates that the worst fears of all those who have spoken out against the slow inexorable growth in the numbers of people visiting Antarctica every year are slowly being realised.

What a wonderful case study it is for the debate about how best to preserve wilderness areas. The 'use it or lose it' camp have long argued that wild places must "pay their way" – particularly in societies where protecting biological diversity is seen as a luxury of the rich, white world. To which the 'use it then lose it' brigade make a simple reply: point us to the evidence that "conservation through exploitation" actually works. Instead, what normally happens is that more people are drawn in until the resource ends up being completely destroyed.

> **Point us to the evidence that conservation through exploitation actually works**

The truth is we're just not very good at allowing nature to pay its way. Politicians and economists have just about got used to the idea of protecting our natural capital when it's a question of resource management, but they still don't get the idea that nature provides us with all sorts of additional services – for free – just so long as the productivity of those natural systems is properly protected.

The bad news is that they're still not catching on fast enough – and that some idiots still think they're helping the environment by building roads across Antarctica.

*BBC Wildlife March 2003*

# HOW TO ANSWER SHORTER QUESTIONS

**You are being asked to follow an argument and select material appropriate to its purpose.**
1. Explain, in your own words, why 'Remote, beautiful and pristine places such as Antarctica' may, in the writer's opinion, one day 'be wildernesses no longer'. *(4 marks)*

## HOW TO ACHIEVE A GOOD MARK

As this question says 'Explain, in your own words', you should:
- **summarise** the arguments **without** copying from the passage or using quotations
- show a **clear understanding** of the points being made
- organise the points in a **logical order** – not just the order given in the text.

> The writer thinks that the wild places in the world will one day be spoilt forever because politicians expect them to make money in return for their protection. In fact, he says politicians should save wilderness areas without expecting them to pay anything in return because nature freely gives our planet so many things for nothing. The author believes there is no evidence that money gained from making use of these areas helps to preserve them; instead he thinks that it simply leads to their destruction.

**Why this is a good response**
This answer:
- shows a clear understanding of the central points of the text, which are given in the student's own words in the opening sentence
- is followed by a brief summary of the arguments, in a logical order, to expand the response and give a full answer to the question.

**You are now being asked to focus on the language of the article.**
2. Examine how the writer's expression affects the reader. *(6 marks)*

## HOW TO ACHIEVE A GOOD MARK

- Look for **evidence** of the **writer's techniques** such as the use of irony, insults, slang, first person (**we**, **us**, **our**), and emotive or figurative language.
- **Analyse** how the writer's language **influences** the reader.
- Select **three good examples** (two marks for each one), each demonstrating different aspects of the writing style. In each case, give the quotation and **identify the effect** the language creates.

POINT 1

> The writer uses a casual, chatty tone in the article, including slang expressions (e.g. 'they still don't get the idea') and clichés (e.g. 'the bad news is'), in order to make him seem like 'one of us', winning the reader to his cause. For example, he begins, 'So now they're going to', which sounds as if he is in the middle of a conversation with the reader.

**Why this is a good response**
This answer:
- shows a sound understanding of the ways in which readers can be affected by a writer's style
- clearly identifies three techniques and analyses them with precision
- uses technical terms, such as 'cliché' and 'first person', accurately and well, which enables the student to be clear and concise
- supports points by appropriate examples from the text.

Using the third person 'they're' creates the effect that the reader and he are on one side, the politicians and economists on the other. This is reinforced later on when he uses the first person, 'we're just not very good', associating the reader with his point of view.

The writer refers to people with different opinions in insulting ways such as, 'some idiots still think'. This has quite a clever effect because no one would admit to agreeing with 'an idiot', so the reader is forced to agree with the writer's point of view.

---

**You are now being asked to focus on the purpose of the article.**
3. What do you consider the writer's intentions and objectives to be? *(5 marks)*

## HOW TO ACHIEVE A GOOD MARK

The two previous questions lead you into this last one, which asks why the writer has written the article. To give a good answer you should:
• **review** the article as a whole
• consider **why** you think it was written
• reflect on **what** you think it achieves and **how** it does so.

The writer aims to inform, offer an argument and persuade the reader in this article. He begins by giving information about the planned building of a road across Antarctica to the South Pole, 'from where the tourists disembark to the very heart of the continent'. This is followed by a warning that it may encourage too many people to visit and therefore spoil the 'remote' and 'pristine' wilderness.

This information provides the basis for the writer's arguments on 'the debate about how best to preserve wilderness areas'. The article argues about the rights and wrongs of making wilderness areas 'pay their way' to provide for conservation and protection.

These two objectives lead to the final and most important purpose of the article, which is to persuade readers, particularly politicians, not to exploit wilderness areas for profit, because by doing so 'the resource ends up being completely destroyed'.

The writer's persuasive, emotive language and arguments work well to convince the reader that only 'idiots' would believe 'that they're helping the environment by building roads across Antarctica'. Nature should be left alone so that it can continue to do what it has always done, 'provide us with all sorts of additional services – for free'.

**Why this is a good response**
This answer:
• recognises that there is more than one purpose to a piece of writing
• gives a clear outline about what each purpose is
• understands how the purposes are related to one another.

## HOW TO COMPARE TEXTS

Often GCSE reading questions will also ask you to make comparisons between texts:

You are now being asked to compare item 1, by Jonathon Porritt, with item 2 from *The Observer*, 'Pick up a penguin'.

Compare:
- what they say
- the language they use.

*(4 marks)*

*Catchy title – playing on an old advertising slogan*

*Enticing, persuasive ideas, encouraging the reader to want to go there*

*Imaginative descriptive, imagery and alliteration to catch the reader's attention*

*Unusual beginning – modern-day expression, like a command*

*Use of second person 'sales pitch' – designed to draw in the reader*

*Persuasive language – modern-day cliché*

# Pick up a penguin

Think pristine white, think ice mountains and deserts of snow. Explorers who conquered Antarctica simply called it The Ice. You can follow in their tracks, forge through the pack-ice, visit research stations in remote islands and see penguins, seals and even whales on an epic voyage this November. You'll travel aboard a Russian icebreaker, Kapitan Khlebnikov, which in 1997 was the first ship to circumnavigate Antarctica with passengers. There is the chance of a lifetime on 24 November, when a solar eclipse will shroud the brutal beauty of the landscape in an eerie Antarctic twilight. Passengers can watch the spectacle in the company of eclipse-chaser and TV pundit Professor John Parkinson.

*Language becomes straightforward giving facts without comment.*

*Cost hidden at the very end of the article*

## The reality

Departing from Port Elizabeth in South Africa on 5 November, the expedition, which ends in Fremantle, Western Australia, on 3 December, costs £15,995 from Wildlife Worldwide (020 8667 9158; www.wildlifeworldwide.com).

*Sunday 26 January 2003*
*The Observer*

## HOW TO ANSWER A QUESTION LIKE THIS

Remember this question carries **4 marks**. The answer needs to:
- be concise
- be very focused
- engage with both texts
- balance points on both sections
- point out similarities and differences
- show understanding of language and purpose.

### COMPARE WHAT THEY SAY:

Both articles are about people visiting Antarctica and they use similar words to describe it: 'Remote, beautiful and pristine' in text 1, 'Think pristine white, think ice mountains and deserts of snow' in text 2.

On the other hand, the attitudes the articles convey are very different. Text 1 suggests that 'making nature pay its way' is a dangerous proposition and that 'the slow inexorable growth in numbers of people visiting Antarctica' must stop to ensure it remains a wilderness area. In contrast, text 2 promotes the opposite point of view by actually encouraging people to come and 'forge through the pack-ice, visit research stations in remote islands'.

### COMPARE THE LANGUAGE THEY USE:

The purpose of both texts is to persuade and naturally both use persuasive language: for example 'nature provides us with all sorts of additional services for free' in text 1 and 'You can follow in their tracks' both persuade the reader by offering them something. Both texts also use modern-day casual expressions such as 'So now they're going to' and 'the chance of a lifetime' to entice the reader and make them feel comfortable.

However, text 1 is also presenting the reader with a point of view through argument, evident in words and phrases such as 'this demonstrates', 'the truth is' and 'point us to some evidence' making it appear more factual. In contrast text 2 is trying to sell a product – a cruise – and therefore uses persuasive phrases such as 'You'll travel aboard', and 'an eerie Antarctic twilight' to win the reader.

**Why this is a good response**
This answer:
- compares the texts in a clearly focused and logical way
- balances points concerning similarities and differences between both articles using supporting evidence from the texts
- the response demonstrates a sound understanding of the texts, their purpose and language.

 To test yourself, go to Reading: Non-fiction – Viewpoint and purpose.

# HOW TO RECOGNISE LITERARY FEATURES AND THEIR EFFECTS

- You need to be able to recognise literary features (also called figurative language) such as metaphors, similes, personification and alliteration.

- You need to understand how these elements work.

- You need to appreciate what they contribute to a piece of writing.

## Here is a typical GCSE question:

**'Under Milk Wood' by Dylan Thomas was originally written as a radio play. This is an extract from the beginning of it. Discuss the way Thomas has used a range of literary features to create particular effects on listeners.**

**In your response you should consider:**
- **figurative language**
- **compound words**
- **alliteration.**

Support your answer with examples from the text.

## HOW TO READ THE TEXT ACTIVELY

- **Analyse** the question to ensure you have fully understood what it is asking you to do (see page 30).

- **Read** the extract carefully.

- **Read** the extract a second time. This time underline or highlight in different colours the language features listed in the question. You do not need to find all of them – just enough to build into your answer.

- **Examine** the points you have picked out and make annotations beside them explaining the effect that these features create.

| Point | Evidence | Comment |
|---|---|---|
| Saying something significant about the feature you have found. | Supporting your point by giving a good example from the text. | Explaining the effect of the example you have given. |

KEY  CONCEPTS

**Figurative language:** language that helps to create an image in the mind of the reader, such as metaphors, similes or personification.

**Compound word:** a word that is created by putting two or more existing words together, e.g. bride's + maid = bridesmaid.

**Alliteration:** the effect created by using the same letter or sound at the beginning of two or more words in succession, e.g. The picky preacher praised the people present.

## HOW TO ANALYSE A TEXT

This text has been annotated to highlight some of its key literary features. In your exam you should not attempt to find more examples in the text than you need to build into your response. Remember – time will be tight!

**Glossary**

1 **courters:** people who are courting – that is, going out with one another
2 **cocklewomen:** women who gather cockleshells from the seashore to sell
3 **trousseaux:** clothes collected by a bride before she marries
4 **anthracite:** a very hard, black coal

[Silence]

**FIRST VOICE** [Very Softly]

To begin at the beginning:

It is spring, moonless night in the small town, starless and **bible-black**, the cobblestreets silent and the **hunched**, **courters'**[1]-and-rabbits' wood **limping** invisible down to the sloeblack, slow, black, crowblack, **fishingboat-bobbing** sea. The houses are **blind as moles** (though moles see fine tonight in the snouting, velvet dingles) or **blind as Captain Cat** there in the muffled middle by the pump and the town clock, the shops in mourning, the Welfare Hall in **widows' weeds**. And all the people of the lulled and dumbfound town are sleeping now.

Hush, the babies are sleeping, the **farmers, the fishers**, the tradesmen and pensioners, cobbler, **schoolteacher, postman and publican**, the undertaker and the fancy woman, **drunkard, dressmaker, preacher, policeman**, the **webfoot cocklewomen**[2] and the tidy wives. Young girls lie bedded soft or glide in their dreams, with rings and trousseaux,[3] **bridesmaided** by glow-worms down the aisles of the **organplaying** wood. The boys are dreaming wicked or of the bucking ranches of the night and the jolly, rodgered sea. And the **anthracite**[4] statues of the horses sleep in the fields, and the cows in the byres, and the dogs in the **wetnosed** yards; and the cats nap in the slant corners or lope sly, streaking and needling, on the **one cloud of the roofs**.

**From _Under Milk Wood_**
**by Dylan Thomas**

---

**Annotations:**

Metaphor – comparing the night with bibles covered in black leather

Personification – the wood is described as bent over and 'limping' down to the sea

Compound words – compressed ideas

Similes – personification of the houses

Alliteration – drawing the attention of the listener

Metaphorical image – making the horses seem very dark and still

Metaphor – making the roofs seem joined together like clouds

**Key**

Figurative language

Compound words

Alliteration

# READING: FICTION

## HOW TO PLAN YOUR RESPONSE

- **Analyse** the question carefully, as has been done below.

- **Connect** what you have discovered through your reading and annotation of the text to the question, including the bullet points.

- **Plan** your response in note form, choosing the best examples and using the question to structure your response.

> Therefore written for sound only – so sounds and images will be important

> Explained in the bullet points

> Talk about

> Use these bullet points to guide and help you plan your response

**'Under Milk Wood' by Dylan Thomas was originally written as a radio play and this is an extract from the beginning of it. Discuss the way he has used a range of literary features in this extract to create particular effects on listeners. In your response you should consider:**
- **figurative language**
- **compound words**
- **alliteration.**

Support your answer with examples from the text.

> The impression created on the audience

---

**Figurative language:** creates strong images, by making comparisons in the minds of listeners.

**Simile:** `the houses are as blind as moles' makes it seem as if the houses look like they cannot see or are unaware of the night around them, which the narrator is describing.

**Metaphors:** `the anthracite statues of the horses' emphasises the stillness and black solidity of the horses at night. This is reinforced by `bible-black' and `one cloud of the roofs'.

**Personification:** `the hunched, courters'-and rabbits' wood limping invisible down' makes the wood seem like an old person bent over, hobbling down to the sea.

**Compound words:** these allow the author to pack ideas together concisely, creating links and more solid images. For example, `webfoot cocklewomen' makes it sound as if their work on the seashore has turned them into seagulls with webbed feet. Also, `cocklewomen' suggests that their job has taken over their identity, as if they have become cockleshells themselves. Two more descriptive compound words are `fishingboat-bobbing' and `organplaying.

**Other language features – alliteration:** `postman and publican' and `drunkard, dressmaker' - Thomas uses alliteration, particularly in the list of people he describes in the second paragraph. This creates a rhythm that makes the list skip along more quickly, and also draws our attention to the contrasts he is making.

## HOW TO WRITE A RESPONSE TO THE QUESTION

- Pick out strong examples to support and illustrate your points.

- You do not have to use or comment on everything you have found.

This extract comes from the beginning of the play and it is clear that Dylan Thomas wants to catch the attention of the audience by using a variety of literary features. As this is a play for the radio rather than the stage, he also uses these features to create images in the minds of his listeners.

He employs a great deal of figurative language - similes, metaphors and personification - to help the audience 'see' what he is describing. Vivid images are created through simile and personification. The phrase 'the houses are as blind as moles' makes it seem as if the houses cannot see what is going on during the night; the curtains are drawn and it is as if their eyelids are closed, making them blind. Later, the metaphor 'the anthracite statues of the horses' creates a strong impression of the stillness and blackness of the horses - they seem more like sculptures and no longer alive. In contrast, in the first paragraph Thomas brings the wood to life through personification. By saying 'the hunched, courters'-and-rabbits' wood limping invisible', the poet makes us think of a furtive, stooped old man, limping down the hill towards the dark sea. Other strong metaphors are 'bible-black', where the listener can picture the night as being as thick and dark as a leather bible, and 'on the one cloud of the roofs', which creates an image of the roofs joined together tightly.

Thomas has packed his ideas together through his use of compound words, some of which, such as 'fishingboat-bobbing' and 'organplaying', he has made up to serve his purpose. Another example, 'the webfoot cocklewomen' makes the women seem as if they have been so taken over by their work that they have become web-footed like the seagulls, or turned into the cockleshells they collect.

Another language feature that the author uses is alliteration. In the second paragraph, alliteration grabs the attention of the listener where Thomas lists the different kinds of villagers who are asleep: 'drunkard, dressmaker, preacher, policeman'. The use of alliteration here also draws our attention to the contrast he is making between the different types of people.

**Why this is a good response**

This answer:
- **makes several relevant points** about the literary features used by the author
- **uses short quotations as evidence** to support the points made
- **comments on** how these features work and the effect they create
- doesn't try to do too much. It **selects** relevant examples to support the points being made, rather than putting in too many different quotations without **commenting on** the effect that they have on listeners.

 To test yourself, go to Reading: Fiction – Literary features and their effects.

# HOW WRITERS CREATE CHARACTER AND ATMOSPHERE

- You need to be able to identify the techniques writers use to establish characters and how they work.

- It is also important to understand how writers create atmosphere and how these methods work.

- You need to appreciate the effect that these two aspects of writing have on the reader.

## This is a GCSE-style question (or part of a question):

In this extract, how has the author conveyed the character of Rashmi to the reader?
In particular you may wish to comment on:
- expression and language
- setting and atmosphere.

Support your answer with examples from the text.

## KEY 🔑 CONCEPTS

**Character:** the personality of an individual in a piece of fiction or non-fiction, as conveyed through:
- their actions
- their words
- their thoughts
- the actions and words of others around them and about them.

**Atmosphere:** the mood of a situation or setting.

## HOW TO READ THE TEXT ACTIVELY

- Read the extract through carefully, making sure that you understand it fully.

- Read it through a second time looking for information that will help you to answer the question.

- Begin to analyse the extract by annotating the points you think are relevant. Use different colours and styles to help you to identify them quickly later on. You could:

  - underline words that give the reader clues about the character of the person: verbs (**sidled, jumped**), adverbs (**uncertainly, painfully**) and adjectives are usually good starting points.

  - highlight key words that convey an atmosphere, such as **screamed** or **thudding**. In some cases, these will be the same as the underlined words.

  - make comments at the side of the page about what you can deduce or learn about the character or atmosphere, perhaps using separate colours for each.

**When you have done this, make sure you can answer these questions.**

What do I know about:
- who the character is?
- her situation?
- her feelings?
- her actions?
- her reaction to others?
- how others react to her?

**Think about how you know these things about the character.**

## HOW TO ANALYSE A TEXT

Annotating the extract will help you
to plan your response more quickly.

*Sounds threatening – why is it happening?*

The knocking began again, and a woman's voice shouted, 'Mr Ray?'

*Atmosphere of wariness*

*Suggests she finds the situation confusing*

Rashmi stood uncertainly, rubbing her knees, wondering what to do. The caller must have heard the noise of the bucket. She sidled into the passage up to the front door, and bent down painfully, stifling a gasp as her back twinged, peering through the metal letterbox cover. She screamed. A pair of dark blue eyes were staring in. Rashmi threw the end of her sari across her head and turned away. 'Is Mr Ray in?' the voice repeated. 'Don't be frightened, I believe you want to learn English. Can I come in?'

*Powerful, short sentence – scream = fear*

*Scary eyes with no face – whose are they?*

*She wants to ignore it and pretend nothing is happening*

*Physical reactions to her situation*

*These words create a feeling of anxiety and suspicion*

Through the thudding in her ears, Rashmi caught the words 'English'. The letterbox was pushed open, and Rashmi jumped as it squeaked. A letter was poked through the slit. Cautiously, suspecting a trap, she reached out and snatched it. Then she opened the envelope. The letter had been typed so she realised the woman had come on official business. Nerving herself, she checked that the door was secured by the chain, and opened a crack to see out without showing herself. A young woman with spiky red hair, white skin, heavy make-up and tight blue jeans stood on the step.

*She locks herself in and others out*

*Shows she is intelligent and able to use her powers of reasoning*

*Contrast with Rashmi's dress – a sari*

They stared at each other for a moment, and the girl began to speak in a low husky voice. Rashmi watched the red mouth in the white face discharging peculiar sounds, repeating, 'Can I come in. Can I come in.' over and over again. The girl put her white hand through the gap in the door and the frame and retrieved the letter, turning it another way and pointing to some sort of heading. Rashmi looked at the picture of a white hand holding a black hand, and pulled her letter back inside the safety of her house. Some English words dredged themselves from her memory. 'Say by-bye.' She closed the door softly and went back to the kitchen, her heart beating loudly.

*Calmer atmosphere, but the stranger is still not trusted or allowed inside*

*Shows she is beginning to think things through more clearly*

**From:** *Salt on the Snow*

**Rukshana Smith**

*Actions show she is still afraid, but calmer now – courageous*

**Key**

Atmosphere

Character (underlined)

## HOW TO PLAN YOUR RESPONSE

Look at the question again. Make sure you know what it is asking you to do.

| How is an important key word |
|---|

| The question is not asking you simply to write about Rashmi's character |

| This means look at why particular words and phrases have been chosen |

| This means, how do these contribute to your understanding of the character? |

**In this extract, <u>how</u> has the author <u>conveyed the character of Rashmi</u> to the reader?**
**In particular you may wish to comment on:**
- **expression and language**
- **setting and atmosphere.**

Support your response with examples from the text.

If there is time, you could make brief notes under the following headings, related to the question, using the information that you have found through your analysis of the extract.

| Powerful verbs | Adverbs | Phrases |
|---|---|---|
| sidled | uncertainly | • wondering what to do |
| twinged | painfully | • stifling a gasp |
| peering | cautiously | • threw the end of her sari across her head and turned away |
| screamed | loudly | |
| frightened | | |
| jumped | | • suspecting a trap |
| thudding | | • nerving herself |
| snatched | | |
| stared | | |

### Setting and atmosphere

- 'The knocking began again' – had been going for some time, makes me wonder why? How long?
- 'Rashmi was 'rubbing her knees'' – suggests she had been kneeling or crouching on the floor to hide – why?
- 'She screamed' – really strong – shows how afraid she was, atmosphere of fear and panic
- 'A pair of dark blue eyes were staring in' – can't see who they belong to, detached and scary.
- 'Suspecting a trap' – Rashmi is thinking more clearly – makes us afraid that it might be one too.
- 'Secured by the chain' – reinforces atmosphere of danger, shows she is thinking things through more carefully.
- 'Discharging peculiar sounds' – reader experiences the sounds as Rashmi does – they don't make sense.
- 'Her heart beating loudly' – ends on a note of triumph, courage over her fear.

## HOW TO WRITE A RESPONSE TO THE QUESTION

**Remember:**
- do not simply write about the character
- focus on **how** (not what)
- use the bullet points to help structure your response.

The setting and atmosphere in this extract, where Rashmi feels as if she is under attack, help the reader to understand her character because we see how she reacts to the situation. The author has developed the character by using powerful words and phrases to describe Rashmi's actions and thoughts. Strong verbs such as 'thudding', 'snatched' and 'stared' help to build the atmosphere, as well as the reader's understanding of the character.

The author creates a threatening atmosphere right from the start with the words 'The knocking began again'. The reader understands the character's confusion through her reactions: 'Rashmi stood uncertainly...wondering what to do', and her fear, 'She sidled into the passage...stifling a gasp'. This shows how she panics when she feels threatened and does not know what to do. Using the short sentence 'She screamed.' has a particularly powerful impact because it shows us Rashmi's terror. This sign of her genuine fear helps the reader to get under the character's skin.

Later, as the fear begins to fade, the author develops other aspects of Rashmi's character, showing Rashmi's intelligence as she behaves 'Cautiously, suspecting a trap'. Her actions become braver, 'Nerving herself, she checked that the door was secured by a chain,' which shows she is thinking logically. This part of Rashmi's character is developed again through her actions, when she looks at the heading on the top of the letter, she remembers the words 'say by-bye' and closes the door so that she can retreat to 'the safety of her house'. The last words, 'her heart beating loudly' show us how shaken she is by the incident, leaving us with a final reminder of her courage.

By using a setting and atmosphere that place Rashmi in what she thinks is a dangerous situation, the author has skilfully developed Rashmi's character through her reactions to this situation.

**Why this is a good response**
This answer:
- shows an understanding of how setting and atmosphere can be used to **develop** aspects of a character
- picks out key words and events **to support points made**
- demonstrates a good appreciation of the character and the **author's purpose**.

 To test yourself, go to Reading: Fiction – Character and atmosphere.

# HOW TO RECOGNISE MOOD AND STYLE

GCSE questions often expect you to understand how an author's style can be used to create a mood or atmosphere in their writing.

To do this you will need to:
- look out for key descriptive words and images
- be sensitive to the use of symbolism – words can operate on two different levels, both on the surface and beneath it.

**This is a GCSE-style question (or part of a question):**

**Explore the ways in which the author has used contrasting moods to create an atmosphere of tension that engages the reader's interest. Examine in particular:**
- **the effect created by images of stagnation and activity**
- **the relationship between the setting and the character's feelings.**

Support your answer with examples from the text.

## HOW TO READ THE TEXT ACTIVELY

- **Begin** by reading the text carefully to make sure that you understand fully what it is about.

- **Then** reread the text, this time underlining in pencil any key words and phrases that describe the setting, atmosphere and feelings.

- **Next**, start to gather information by analysing the text more closely. Highlight the negative images of stagnation in one colour and those relating to activity in another.

- **Examine** these contrasting words and images and make notes on the effects they create in terms of mood and atmosphere.

- Look at the images and think about whether they might also represent something else 'beneath the surface of the words' – that is, symbolism.

KEY 🔑 CONCEPTS

> **Mood:** the feeling created by the writer through words that reflect emotions and sensations, for example sunlight suggests positive feelings such as happiness or joy.
>
> **Symbolism:** the way writers use words to suggest meanings beneath the surface; for example a mist can mean a physical fog, but can also be symbolic of a character's confused thoughts.
>
> **Imagery:** the use of language (often figurative language) to create a vivid picture in the reader's mind.

## HOW TO ANALYSE THE TEXT

Annotating the text like this will help
you to plan your response.

**Negative mood of stillness and despair**

**'Fetters' and 'uniform' linked with captivity**

**Repetition**

**Negative images – gloomy mood**

**Positive images creating exciting atmosphere and action**

**Keyword used to suggest she is on the edge of something**

**Contrast between outside and inside the house**

**Tension between calm life and a struggle**

**Positive natural images – positive mood, symbolic of breaking free to explore distant places**

**Why – what will happen?**

I did not like re-entering Thornfield. To pass its threshold was to return to stagnation; to cross the silent hall, to ascend the darksome staircase, to seek my own little lonely room, and then to meet tranquil Mrs Fairfax, and spend the long winter evening with her, and her only, was to quell wholly the faint excitement wakened by my walk – to slip again over my faculties the viewless fetters[1] of an uniform and too still existence, whose very privileges of security and ease I was becoming incapable of appreciating. What good it would have done me at that time to have been tossed in the storms of an uncertain struggling life, and to have been taught by rough and bitter experience to long for the calm amidst which I now repined!…[2]

I lingered at the gates; I lingered on the lawn; I paced backwards and forwards on the pavement; the shutters of the glass door were closed; I could not see into the interior; and both my eyes and spirit seemed drawn from the gloomy house – from the grey hollow filled with rayless cells, as it appeared to me – to that sky expanded before me, a blue sea absolved from taint of cloud; the moon ascending it in solemn march; her orb seeming to look up as she left the hill-tops, from behind which she had come, far and further below her, and aspired to the zenith,[3] midnight dark in its fathomless[4] depth and measureless distance; and for those trembling stars that followed her course; they made my heart tremble, my veins glow when I viewed them. Little things recall us to earth; the clock struck in the hall; that sufficed; I turned from moon and stars, opened a side-door, and went in.

**From *Jane Eyre* by Charlotte Brontë**

**Key**

Negative images
linked with
stagnation

Positive images
linked with activity
and excitement

———

Key words
(underlined)

Glossary
1 fetters: chains that bind a prisoner
2 repined: to feel sad and miserable
3 zenith: highest point
4 fathomless: bottomless, without depth

## HOW TO PLAN YOUR RESPONSE

- Make sure that you understand what the question is asking you to do.

- Underline the key words in the question and use these to guide your response.

- Draw out points from your analysis of the text that will help you to answer the question in a logical way.

---

Investigate or talk about

Pick out different examples and show how they are different to one another

Link examples to this part of the question to show how the author creates tension

**Explore** the ways in which the author has used <u>contrasting moods</u> to create an <u>atmosphere of tension</u> that engages the reader's interest.
Examine in particular:
- the effect created by images of stagnation and activity
- the relationship between the setting and the character's feelings.

Support your answer with examples from the text.

**Contrasting moods**

| Stagnation | Activity |
|---|---|
| silent hall | faint excitement wakened |
| darksome staircase | tossed in the storms of an uncertain struggling life |
| tranquil Mrs Fairfax | paced backwards and forwards |
| long winter evening | sky expanded |
| calm amidst which I now repined | blue sea |
| lingered, lingered | moon ascending |
| gloomy house | orb seeming to look up |
| grey hollow | left the hill-tops |
| rayless cell | made my heart tremble, my veins glow |
| recall us to earth | turned from the moon and stars |

**Tension**

- inside the house/outside world – moon and stars
- dark, silent, gloomy/excitement, trembling, measureless, glow
- known/unknown
- security/struggle
- inactivity/movement

## HOW TO WRITE A RESPONSE

This is an open-ended task that does not ask a direct question, but expects you to discuss the effect of the examples you have chosen.

You will still need to have:
- an introduction showing you understand the question
- at least two paragraphs 'exploring' contrast, mood and atmosphere
- a conclusion saying how the images engage the reader in the text.

In this extract the author has used a number of negative and positive images, which help to create a tense atmosphere. The negative images, mainly to do with the character's return to the 'too still existence' of the 'gloomy' house, are set against more positive images about the tempting excitement of the unknown world that lies beyond. The contrast between these two opposites creates a feeling of tension.

The extract begins with a negative mood, with the words 'I did not like' and a 'return to stagnation', followed by images of the house as being a 'darksome', 'silent' place inhabited by a 'tranquil' woman. The contrast between this and the outside world is shown by the word 'threshold', which represents both the actual doorway and being on the edge between one existence and another.

This idea is also explored through the narrator's comparison of the 'too still existence', which she feels bound to by 'fetters' and the 'excitement wakened by my walk'. She sets the 'privileges of security' against being 'tossed in the storms of an uncertain struggling life'. Further tension between these two comes when she says that past experiences have made her long for the calm, which she now wants to reject.

In the second paragraph the author creates tension by making the narrator choose between staying outside and going in. The inside of the house is described as shuttered and 'closed', whereas outside 'the sky expanded' becoming 'a blue sea' over which the moon shines above a 'fathomless depth and measureless distance'.

I find the clear contrast between these images and the tension they create between the two worlds powerful and interesting. They make me wonder why the narrator 'turned from the moon and stars' and what will happen as a result.

### Why this is a good response
This answer:
- shows an understanding of the terms mood, tension, contrast and atmosphere which have been applied to the text in making the response
- gives 'pin-pointed' examples to illustrate accurate, interesting points
- offers a personal response that indicates a genuine engagement with the text.

To test yourself, go to Reading: Fiction – Mood and style.

# HOW TO REVISE POETRY

- For GCSE English, you have to study a variety of different kinds of poetry for coursework, for your exam or sometimes for both.

- If the poetry you have studied is in one of your English exams, you will need to revise what you have learned during the course.

- This unit will help you to structure your revision. Later units will focus on helping you to answer exam questions.

## KEY 🔑 CONCEPTS

> **Theme:** the subject matter or topic of the poetry.
>
> **Voice:** the narrator or person speaking in the poem – which may or may not be the poet. Don't assume the voice of the poem is the poet's. Sometimes poets write from a different perspective, speaking as someone else.

## THINKING ABOUT POETRY

- Start by completing **charts** of all the poems/poets that you have studied for the exam. (The chart is available on the CD-ROM.)

- Some headings have been suggested. You can change the headings to suit your poems. For example:

| Name of poem | 'Limbo' |
|---|---|
| Name of poet | Kamau Brathwaite |
| Country of origin | Barbados, Caribbean |
| Subject (in no more than 10 words) | Slaves 'dance' on ships from Africa – uplifted by music |
| Voice | First person |
| Tense | Present |
| Poem's structure | Free verse with stanzas and a refrain |
| Setting | Slave ship – about 200 years ago |

- Gather together clean copies of each poem to make **notes** on.

- Review what you have learned about each poem. Think about the **links** between them usig the second chart on the CD-ROM. For example:

| The poem | The poet | Country | Conflict | Contrasts | Culture/ religion | Happiness | Hardship/ suffering |
|---|---|---|---|---|---|---|---|
| Limbo | Brathwaite | Barbados | ✓ | ✓ | ✓ | ✓ | ✓ |
| Nothing's Changed | Afrika | South Africa | ✓ | ✓ | | ✓ | |
| Island Man | Nichols | Guyana | | ✓ | | ✓ | |
| Blessing | Dharker | Pakistan | | | | | ✓ |
| | | | | | | | |

- **Test yourself** by taking another clean copy of a poem. **Highlight** particular words/lines and add annotations (see pages 42–43).

## THINGS TO LOOK OUT FOR WHEN REVISING A POEM

### First impressions

- **Form a first impression** of the poem by simply looking at it, its **shape and visual features**. Does it have long or short lines, or perhaps a mixture? What effect does this have on you as a reader? Does the poem have regular or irregular stanzas, or none at all?

- **What does the title tell you** about the poem's meaning and what it conveys? (Later, think about why the poet chose the title and its relationship to the poem that follows.)

- **How has the poet used punctuation** such as capital letters and full stops? Are they in places you would expect them to be? If not, what effect does this create? Why has the poet has chosen to ignore them?

- **Are there any other presentational effects** such as italics or bold or capitals? If so, why are they there? What effect do they have?

### Listen to the poem

- In order to get the best out of a poem, you really need to read it two or three times (at least once out loud if you can).

- Try to develop a feel for the rhythm of the poem.

- Listen to the sounds that the words in the poem create. (Harsh letters like 't' or 'k' create a different feeling from softer ones like 's' or 'm'.)

- Does the poem rhyme? If so, does it do so in a regular pattern or just 'by chance'? Or does it have an internal rhyme in the middle of a line? What effect do rhymes create?

- What mood or atmosphere is created by the poem? How do you feel as you read the poem? Think about how this is created – is it the sound, what is being said or both?

### Poetic features

Look out for particular poetic features; some will be more obvious than others in different poems. Some examples are:

- **structure or form** – the way a poem is 'built', that is its stanzas, line length, punctuation, etc.

- **language** – the words, phrases and expressions that a poet chooses to use in the poem, often because of the sounds or associations they may have (this doesn't happen by chance, the poet makes deliberate choices).

- **alliteration** – the repetition of a particular sound, e.g.'limbo like'.

- **repetition** – words, whole lines or even several lines may be repeated to create emphasis, rhythm or pace .

- **imagery** – the picture that a poet creates. This could be a straightforward description using a single word or phrase like 'long dark deck'. Or it could be a symbolic suggestion such as 'the dumb gods are raising me'. We can picture this in our minds, but it isn't really happening.

- **figurative language** – other forms of imagery such as metaphor, simile, or personification. You need to think about the effect created.

- **theme** – the message or what the poet wants to say and why it was written in the first place!

All the language features mentioned above simply help to make the poem's meaning stronger or clearer.

## HOW TO ANNOTATE A POEM

Some annotations have been added to the poem below to show you the types of things you could highlight and the kinds of comments that you could make.

*Long lines in the poem are like the stick held during the limbo dance*

*This word is repeated many times in the poem – this creates the mood*

*Repetition – this creates the harsh sound of stick used as a whip*

*Refrain repeated throughout the poem – a chant like the beat of the drums*

*Key message of the poem – repeated for emphasis*

*Describes the action of the limbo dance as the dancer bends backwards*

**Limbo**

And limbo stick is the silence in front of me
*limbo*

*limbo*
*limbo like me*
*limbo*
*limbo like me*

long dark night is the silence in front of me
*limbo*
*limbo like me*

stick hit sound
and the ship like it ready

stick hit sound
and the dark still steady

*limbo*
*limbo like me*

long dark deck and the water surrounding me
long dark deck and the silence is over me

*limbo*
*limbo like me*

stick is the whip
and the dark deck is slavery

stick is the whip
and the dark deck is slavery

*limbo*
*limbo like me*

drum stick knock
and the darkness is over me

knees spread wide
and the water is hiding me

*limbo*
*limbo like me*

**Limbo** – this word has three meanings in the poem:
1. It is a place between heaven and hell where the souls of the dead go and from which they cannot escape.
2. It refers to the dark hold of the slave ship where the slaves are kept in chains as they make their journey from Africa to America.
3. It is the dance that slaves were made to do using a stick, to make them exercise on the journey. It is now a popular Caribbean dance during which the dancer has to bend backwards to go underneath a horizontal bar which is lowered nearer and nearer to the ground.

*Describes the slave ship and the ocean around the narrator*

# READING: POETRY

*'Down' is both going down in the dance and going down to the ship's hold*

*Provides the beat for the exercise/dance*

*Key line – this shows change and hope, indicating that spirits are lifted by the music*

*'Dumb' because they no longer speak to him*

*Irony – the dance and the music gave the slaves something to live for on their horrific journey*

knees spread wide
and the dark ground is under me

down
down
down

and the drummer is calling me

limbo
limbo like me

sun coming up
and the drummers are praising me

out of the dark
and the dumb gods are raising me

up
up
up

and the music is saving me

hot
slow
step

on the burning ground.

***Kamau Brathwaite***

*Contrasts with 'down' above*

*Strong words and image to end with – hot like hell*

The poem:
- has strong rhythm reflecting the beat of the dance
- is like a chant or a song
- brings drama of the subject to life
- shows strength of slaves who made the dance their own – symbolic of their protest against what happened to them
- is written for performance.

**Kamau Brathwaite** was born 1930 in Barbados and became Professor of Comparative Literature, New York. A Caribbean writer, he is also poet of world status winning many awards for his work.

 To help you revise Poetry, go to Poetry Revision Chart.

# HOW TO WRITE ABOUT A POEM

This GCSE-style question could be adapted for many of the poems you have studied:

**Discuss how the poet Nissim Ezekiel conveys his attitudes and feelings in the poem 'Night of the Scorpion'. In particular focus on:**

- the poet's use of language and form
- what the poem reveals about his culture and beliefs.

## ANALYSING A POEM

Start by taking a clean copy of the poem and annotating it. Using different-coloured pens for the annotation can help you sort out your ideas into:

- language and form
- culture and beliefs.

You are looking for examples that reveal the poet's attitudes and beliefs. You do not need to find everything – just enough to use in your response.

**Remember!**

- A question like this is not expecting you to retell what happens in the poem.
- You must decide **what** attitudes and feelings are revealed in the poem and **how** they are conveyed.
- A response that simply retells the story, or says what the poem is about, will not gain many marks.

## KEY ⟭══ CONCEPTS

**Culture:** the way of life and customs of a society.

**Belief:** the religion and/or superstitions of a person or society.

**Form:** the structure of a poem and the way it has been written, for example using stanzas or free verse, rhyme patterns a or rhythm.

**Language:** the words and expressions used in a poem, which may include the use of dialect, as well as words chosen for their sound.

Poet Nissim Ezekiel was born in India in 1924 of Jewish parents. After many varied and interesting jobs, he became Professor of English at Bombay University. He has been described by some as 'India's greatest living poet'.

## HOW TO ANNOTATE A POEM

**Key**

Language and form

Culture and beliefs

*Free verse/first-person narrative – sounds like a conversation*

*Link with the devil*

*Vivid image – the child was probably frightened*

*Repetition of 'May' makes it sound like a prayer or chant*

*'They said' makes it seem as if he was not part of the action and did not believe in it*

*Repetition to create emphasis*

*Repetition – the child was not part of what was going on but was watching*

*Contrast of short verse – mother is calm after all the commotion. Child admires her.*

**Night of the Scorpion**

I remember the night my mother
was stung by a scorpion. Ten hours
of steady rain had driven him
to crawl beneath a sack of rice.
Parting with his poison – flash
of diabolic tail in the dark room –
he risked the rain again.
The peasants came like swarms of flies
and buzzed the name of God a hundred times
to paralyse the Evil One.
With candles and with lanterns
throwing giant scorpion shadows
on the mud-baked walls
they searched for him: he was not found.
They clicked their tongues.
With every movement that the scorpion made
his poison moved in Mother's blood, they said.
May he sit still, they said.
May the sins of your previous birth
be burned away tonight, they said.
May your suffering decrease
the misfortunes of your next birth, they said.
May the sum of evil
balanced in this unreal world
against the sum of good
become diminished by your pain.
May the poison purify your flesh
of desire, and your spirit of ambition,
they said, and they sat around
on the floor with my mother in the centre,
the peace of understanding on each face.
More candles, more lanterns, more neighbours,
more insects, and the endless rain.
My mother twisted through and through,
groaning on a mat.
My father, sceptic, rationalist,
trying every curse and blessing,
powder, mixture, herb and hybrid.
He even poured a little paraffin
upon the bitten toe and put a match to it.
I watched the flame feeding on my mother.
I watched the holy man perform his rites
to tame the poison with an incantation.
After twenty hours
it lost its sting.

My mother only said
Thank God the scorpion picked on me
and spared my children.
*Nissim Ezekiel*

*Simile – image of the people like insects. Negative image. Perhaps the child didn't like them?*

*Another link between the scorpion and the devil*

*Villagers believe the scorpion's movements would cause pain to the victim*

*Hindus believe in the reincarnation of the spirit, and that suffering in one life helps to purify you in the next*

*Child is not part of this*

*Harsh-sounding words – his father didn't really believe but went along with it*

*Alliteration – cruel, painful action of the flame. Child seems critical of father?*

## HOW TO PLAN YOUR RESPONSE

Review what the question has asked you to do and highlight the key words in the question.

If there are bullet points that give you guidance on what to put in your answer, then use them to plan your response. If there are no bullets, you may find it useful to create your own to give you a clear focus when writing your response.

**Form**
- Free verse – as if the poet/narrator is talking to you
- First-person narrative voice – sounds like someone telling a story
- Repetition – gives a strong rhythm and builds up tension
- Short last verse – strong contrast with long first verse.

**Language**
- Some religious language – almost like a prayer or a chant
- Figurative language – simile: peasants are 'like swarms of flies'; onomatopoeia: 'buzzed'
- Metaphor – scorpion is a devil: 'diabolic tail' and 'the Evil One'
- Some harsh-sounding words, e.g. 'sceptic, rationalist'.

**Culture and beliefs**
- Looks at mixture of superstition and religious belief
- Belief of the villagers – suffering in one life will purify you in the next
- Superstition – any movement of the scorpion will move the poison in the victim's blood
- Contrast in beliefs between the peasants and the father – but the father will try anything to save his wife.

**Feelings and attitudes**
- The narrator is looking back on an event in his childhood which frightened him – powerful images of the night and the scorpion
- He did not feel a part of all the activity – 'I watched' and 'they sat around on the floor with my mother in the centre'
- He knew what the peasants were doing but did not take part in all the superstitious rites – 'they said' – and he probably didn't believe in them
- He was aware of the struggle going on in his father – 'sceptic, rationalist' – but he still tried every 'curse and blessing'. Narrator is possibly critical of his father – 'he even poured a little paraffin'
- Poet admired the way his mother is so calm and unselfish when she recovers – 'My mother only said'.

## HOW TO WRITE A RESPONSE TO THE QUESTION

**Remember to:**
- focus on **how** the poet tells us about his **attitudes** and **feelings**, especially in relation to those outlined in the bullet points
- support your points with **quotations** or close reference to the poem
- offer **your own** ideas and thoughts.

In 'Night of the Scorpion', Nissim Ezekiel uses an emotional story to show his attitudes and feelings. By writing in free verse, he can describe the dramatic events of 'the night my mother was stung by a scorpion' in an almost casual, conversational style. The first-person narration through a child's eyes ('I remember', 'I watched') makes the poem personal and real.

The poet uses straightforward but colourful language, so we can imagine the scene quite clearly. The villagers, with their candles and lanterns, throwing 'giant scorpion shadows on the mud-baked walls' create a sinister mood. It is as if the 'Evil One' really is watching them.

The poet shows his attitude to the peasants and their beliefs through the simile 'The peasants came like swarms of flies' who 'buzzed the name of God a hundred times'. Although this creates a humorous picture, the word 'peasants' tells us that the poet feels that they, and their beliefs, are somehow inferior, which is a central part of the poem.

This sense of feeling apart is strengthened by the repetition of 'May...they said' three times – as the peasants chant their prayers for the mother, believing that suffering in one life helps to purify a person in the next. However, the narrator is not joining in; the child is on the outside looking in, rather than being one of them. This is emphasised by the repetition of 'I watched' and by the image 'they sat around on the floor with my mother in the centre'. The child is not sitting with them; he is not part of it.

The poet is quite critical of the father's attempts to join in with the peasants despite his being 'sceptic, rationalist' – harsh-sounding words. The poet says 'he even poured a little paraffin', which sounds as though the child could not believe what lengths the father was prepared to go to to save his wife.

In contrast, the poet admires his mother. She is calm and unselfish. Ezekiel expresses her strength and courage in the quiet conclusion after all the commotion: 'Thank God the scorpion picked on me'.

**Why this is a good response**

This answer:
- discusses **form** and **language**
- shows a good understanding of the **attitudes** and **feelings** conveyed
- comments on **culture** and **beliefs**
- uses quotations effectively.

 To test yourself, go to Reading: Poetry – Writing about a poem.

# HOW TO COMPARE POEMS 1

- Many GCSE exam questions expect you to compare poems.

- You may need to comment on the theme of the poems, or on the mood or tone.

- You will need to look for similarities and differences between the poems.

- Focus your analysis on the language, expression and style of the poems, as well as their cultural heritage.

## HINTS ON COMPARING POEMS

### Dos:

- Consider subject, structure, theme, mood or language, making short notes next to each annotation.
- Think about whether the voice of the poems (e.g. I, you, she) are the same or different.
- Consider whether the poems have the same purpose.
- Compare the culture and beliefs expressed in the poems.
- Make notes about points that are different by highlighting or underlining in different colours so they stand out from |the similarities.
- Find evidence (quotations or close references) from the poems to support the points that you want to make.
- Introduce your response by giving an overview of the poems and a few general comments about their relationship with one another.
- Write in a logical order, putting the similarities first and then the differences.
- Include a representative balance of differences and similarities.
- Summarise the main points you have made in a conclusion.
- Make sure that you have answered any direct questions the task has given you.

### Don'ts:

- Don't expect the poems to be exactly the same!
- Avoid getting too involved in the 'story' or content of the poem.
- Try not to write about everything – select the best points.
- Don't use a quotation more than once if you can avoid it.
- Don't assume a poem is always about the poet's personal experiences.
- Don't presume that the voice of the poem is the poet's just because it is written in the first person.
- Avoid repeating words and phrases too often.
- Don't focus too much on just one poem – make sure there is a balance between the two.

This GCSE question asks you to make a comparison between two poems that have a similar mood:

**Compare the ways in which the poets write about their changing world in 'This Room' and one other poem of your choice from those you have studied.**

## HOW TO CHOOSE ANOTHER POEM FOR COMPARISON

Before you can start to answer this question, you will need to consider carefully which poem you will choose to compare with the one given in the question.

If, during your revision, you created a chart like the one suggested on page 40, it will help you to remember poems that can be paired together because of their similarities.

In this case, the question refers to 'change', so you need to consider which poems are about a changing world. If you are following the AQA A specification, for example, you could compare 'Nothing's Changed', 'Blessing', 'Love after Love' or 'Hurricane Hits England' to 'This Room'. Of these, the best choice would be 'Hurricane Hits England' because:

- it has a similar theme – the idea of things literally being uprooted and thrown in the air
- there are many parallels in the language and expression of the two poems
- there are also several differences which can provide interesting points for discussion.

### How to begin

- If possible, place the two poems side by side so that you can see them both at the same time.
- Quickly reread them to remind yourself of the content.
- Highlight and annotate lines that are similar to one another.
- Highlight and annotate lines that are different .

KEY CONCEPTS

**Similarities:** aspects that are alike or have a connection between them.

**Differences:** aspects that are not alike or where another approach is taken.

## HOW TO HIGHLIGHT AND ANNOTATE

Some annotations have been added to the poems below to show you the types of things you could highlight and the kinds of comments that you could make.

**Key**

Similarities

Differences

**This Room**

This room is breaking out
of itself, cracking through
its own walls
in search of space, light,
empty air.

*Human beings not in control*

The bed is lifting out of
its nightmares.
From dark corners, chairs
are rising up to crash through clouds.

*Their world is turned upside down*

This is the time and place
to be alive:
when the daily furniture of our lives
stirs, when the improbable arrives.
Pots and pans bang together
in celebration, clang
past the crowd of garlic, onions, spices,
fly by the ceiling fan.
No one is looking for the door.

*Excitement and freedom expressed*

In all this excitement
I'm wondering where
I've left my feet, and why

my hands are outside, clapping.

*Imtiaz Dharker*

*Exhilaration and joy, freedom arising from change*

**Imtiaz Dharker**
Born in Lahore in 1954. Although she grew up in Britain, she now lives in India. She published her first book *Purdah and Other Poems* in 1989, and her second, *Postcards from God*, in 1994.

## Hurricane Hits England

**Grace Nichols**
Born in Georgetown, Guyana in 1950. She grew up in a small coastal village and later moved to the city. Since 1977 she has lived in the UK. She has worked as a teacher and journalist and also has a strong interest in Guyanese folk tales. Her first poetry collection, published in 1983, won the Commonwealth Poetry Prize. *I is a Long-Memoried Woman*, published in 1983, won the Commonwealth Poetry Prize.

**Opening lines make strong statements**

It took a hurricane, to bring her closer
To the landscape.
Half the night she lay awake,
The howling ship of the wind,
Its gathering rage,
Like some dark ancestral spectre.
Fearful and reassuring.

**References to Carib and African gods, and previous hurricane**

Talk to me Huracan
Talk to me Oya
Talk to me Shango
And Hattie,
My sweeping, back-home cousin.

**Time and place**

Tell me why you visit
An English coast?
What is the meaning
Of old tongues
Reaping havoc
In new places?

**Imagery different – one natural the other manufactured**

The blinding illumination,
Even as you short-
Circuit us
Into further darkness?

What is the meaning of trees
Falling heavy as whales
Their crusted roots
Their cratered graves?

O why is my heart unchained?

**Repetition and use of first-person voice**

Tropical Oya of the Weather,
I am aligning myself to you,
I am following the movement of your winds,
I am riding the mystery of your storm.

Ah, sweet mystery,
Come to break the frozen lake in me,
Shaking the foundations of the very trees within me,
Come to let me know
That the earth is the earth is the earth.

*Grace Nichols*

## HOW TO PLAN

Following your annotation of the poems, draw out the main points in a brief list.

| Similarities | Differences |
|---|---|
| • Free verse with irregular stanzas.<br>• First-person poems.<br>• Opening lines make a strong statement.<br>• Similar themes – turmoil bringing about change.<br>• Images of upheaval in the poet's world – some lines very alike in terms of the ideas they express.<br>• End with a feeling of freedom and change. | • 'Hurricane' refers to the poet's heritage, culture and beliefs – 'This Room' doesn't.<br>• 'Hurricane' has sense of place – 'This Room' could be set anywhere.<br>• 'Hurricane' describes a natural event with imagery from the natural world – 'This Room' is symbolic and surreal with manufactured household objects. |

## HOW TO WRITE YOUR RESPONSE

• Begin with an introduction that:

1 states which poem you have chosen for comparison;

2 indicates briefly general similarities between the poems;

3 quickly introduces general differences that you have found.

> [1] Imtiaz Dharker's poem 'This Room' is about turmoil and change, which is a theme that is also present in 'Hurricane Hits England' by Grace Nichols. [2] Both poems explore the idea of how people react to the world about them being thrown into confusion. [3] However, 'Hurricane' has a definite sense of time, place and culture, whereas 'This Room' could apply to anyone, anywhere in the world.

• Then begin to examine the similarities that you have found between the two poems.

4 Comments on aspects such as **structure** and **voice** could provide a straightforward starting point.

> [4] The two poems have a similar structure, both being written in free verse with lines and stanzas of varying, irregular lengths. This makes them easy to read. As they are also both written in the first person, 'our lives' and 'short-circuit us', it sounds as if the poets are speaking directly to the reader. Both poems begin with strong opening lines: 'This room is breaking out of itself' and
>
> 'It took a hurricane, to bring her closer
> To the landscape.'
>
> Both of these openings introduce the reader directly to the theme of the poems.

5 Move on to points concerned with **content** and **themes**.

> [5] The two poems both describe a world where human beings have lost control of their environment:
>
> 'The bed is lifting out of
> its nightmares' ('This Room')
> and

'The howling ship of the wind,
Its gathering rage' ('Hurricane Hits England').

In both cases, this causes an emotional response and reaction from the reader. In 'This Room', the poet says,

'This is the time and place
to be alive:'

and Nichols says, 'O why is my heart unchained?' The lines almost echo each other in the sense of freedom that they express.

[6] Towards the end, both poets comment on their experiences, which is emphasised through the repetition of the word 'I' at the beginning of the lines:

'I'm wondering where
I've left my feet, and why

my hands are outside
clapping'

('This Room')

'I am aligning myself to you,
I am following the movement of
your winds,
I am riding the mystery of your
storm.'

('Hurricane Hits England')

This focus on the first person
helps the reader to share the poets' feelings as they express their individual conclusions: Dharker is jubilant, although she can't explain why; Nichols is waiting for

'sweet mystery,
Come to break the frozen lake in me,
Shaking the foundations of the very trees within me'.

Both poets convey the freedom and change that has come as a result of what has happened to them.

**6** As far as you can, deal with points **in the order in which they occur** in the poems.

Next, write about the contrasts and differences between the poems. In this case:

7 the sense of place in 'Hurricane Hits England', that is missing in 'The Room'

8 the different cultural perspective of the poems

9 the contrasting imagery used – natural versus manufactured.

[7] Although the poems have many similarities, there are also important differences. One of the most striking is the sense of place and time. 'Hurricane Hits England' is set following the great storm which hit England one night in 1987, which provides Nichols with a very definite time and place:

'Tell me why you visit
An English coast?'

Dharker's poem, on the other hand, is not strongly linked to a particular time and the indirect reference to 'the crowd of garlic, onions, spices' flying past a 'ceiling fan' is all that gives this poem any sense of place.

[8] The two poems are also different in terms of their cultural perspective. 'This Room' is not tied to any particular belief or culture. In contrast, 'Hurricane Hits England' refers to the ancient Carib god of the wind 'Huracan' and the storm gods 'Oya' and 'Shango' from West Africa, giving a strong reminder of the slave trade and the heritage from which the poem springs.

[9] Perhaps the most striking difference between the two poems is in the imagery that the poets have used. 'Hurricane Hits England' is about a natural event, whereas 'This Room' describes something surreal. As a result, the images in 'Hurricane' are linked with natural features such as 'trees Falling heavy as whales', whereas in 'This Room' the images are concerned with manufactured objects, 'the daily furniture of our lives', such as 'pots and pans'.

Finally bring your answer to a **conclusion** in which you:

**10 draw together** the points you have raised

**11** make a **personal observation** regarding the poems.

[10] From these points it can be seen that 'Hurricane Hits England' and 'This Room' are different in the imagery they use and their cultural roots. However, the themes and ideas in the poems have strong similarities. In both, the poet's world is turned 'topsy turvy' as change comes into their lives:

'Reaping havoc
In new places' ('Hurricane')
and
'From dark corners; Chairs
are rising up to crash through clouds.' ('This Room').

[11] I like the way in which both poems celebrate the change that has been brought about, 'cracking through its own walls' and 'Shaking the foundations of the very trees within' them.

**Why this is a good response**

This answer:
- has a **clear structure**
- shows that the poems have **similarities and differences**
- makes **close reference** to the poems by using a number of quotations
- demonstrates a **sound understanding** of the poems through observations and personal remarks.

 To test yourself, go to Reading: Poetry – Comparing poems: Similarities and differences.

# HOW TO COMPARE POEMS 2

- This unit gives you more guidance on how to answer a GCSE question that asks you to compare two poems.

- The question and the poems are quite challenging but if you can understand these, then it will give you confidence going into your exam.

**This is a GCSE-style question:**

**Compare 'Vultures' by Chinua Achebe with one other poem to show how poets use poetry to make a protest.**

## HOW TO ANSWER THIS QUESTION

**Begin** by reminding yourself about the content and style of the poem named.

**Next,** review the poems that you have studied and think about which ones relate to the poem you have been given. In this case, ask yourself which other poems:
- make a protest
- are concerned with people's inhumanity to other people
- consider the responsibility of one human being to another
- could be described as political
- provoke the reader by asking questions.

**Draw** up a short list. You might consider choosing 'Limbo', 'Not My Business' or 'What Were They Like?' for comparison.

**Choose** one of these poems by considering which would provide the most interesting comparisons with the given poem. It could be one that deals with a similar subject in a very different way or one that comes from a similar or different culture that gives the same message. In this case we have chosen 'Not My Business', a poem by another Nigerian poet.

**Annotate** both poems, paying particular attention to those features that relate to the question.

**Make links** between the two poems by drawing up a quick chart headed 'Similarities' and 'Differences'.

**KEY** 🔑 **CONCEPTS**

> **Protest:** to make an objection or show a disagreement, often political, usually through some kind of statement or action.

**Plan** your response, including:
- an introduction – outlining the two poems very briefly in relation to the task
- discussion on the similarities
- discussion on the differences
- your overall conclusions in relation to the task.

# READING: POETRY

## HOW TO ANALYSE THESE POEMS

*Scavengers feeding off others*

*Striking images – violence, ugliness (like Belsen)*

*Break – signals change in focus*

*Strong, powerful and horrific image*

**Vultures**

In the greyness
and drizzle of one despondent[1]
dawn unstirred by harbingers[2]
of sunbreak a vulture
perching high on broken
bone of a dead tree
nestled close to his
mate his smooth
bashed-in head, a pebble
on a stem rooted in
a dump of gross
feathers, inclined affectionately
to hers. Yesterday they picked
the eyes of a swollen
corpse in a water-logged
trench and ate the
things in its bowel. Full
gorged they chose their roost
keeping the hollowed remnant
in easy range of cold
telescopic eyes…
    Strange
indeed how love in other
ways so particular
will pick a corner
in that charnel-house[3]
tidy it and coil up there, perhaps
even fall asleep – her face
turned to the wall!
… Thus the Commandant at Belsen[4]
Camp going home for
the day with fumes of
human roast clinging
rebelliously to his hairy
nostrils will stop
at the wayside sweet-shop
and pick up a chocolate
for his tender offspring
waiting at home for Daddy's
return…

*Contrasting, almost touching, images of tenderness between the two birds*

*Gruesome image of what the birds feed on for their survival*

*Accurate image of vultures' eyes – also reminder of the fact that we are all always being watched by other 'vultures' in society*

*Image of death again*

*Turning a blind eye to the horror around her*

*His body will not give up the smell – the reminder of what he has been doing 'at work'*

*Contrast – even the 'Belsen butcher' – how can he do this?*

### Glossary
1 **despondent:** miserable, dismal
2 **harbinger:** omen, messenger
3 **charnel-house:** vault where dead bodies are deposited
4 **Belsen:** Nazi concentration camp in WW2
5 **bounteous:** plenteous, generous
6 **providence:** fate, divine intervention
7 **encapsulated:** enclosed, summarised
8 **perpetuity:** eternity, without end

# READING: POETRY

Ironic tone here?

Chilly image – alliteration and harsh sounds

### Chinua Achebe
Nigerian poet and novelist born 1930. Well known for raising his voice in protest against evil and corrupt regimes.

Praise bounteous[5]
providence[6] if you will
that grants even an ogre
a tiny glow-worm
tenderness encapsulated[7]
in icy caverns of a cruel
heart or else despair
for in the very germ
of that kindred love is
lodged the perpetuity[8]
of evil.

*Chinua Achebe*

Powerful ending to the poem, asking questions. Think about the balance of good and evil. Can evil people be capable of good? Can they only love their own offspring – 'that kindred love?' – who will ensure that their evil lives after them?

Theme of the poem

Third person – impersonal, unknown – threatening tone

Hunger is a real fear in some African countries

Repeated – increasing the threatening tone

No way to question – no way to fight back

Stark image of frozen fear

Threatening repetition of 'waiting' and the word 'silence'

**Not My Business**
They picked Akanni up one morning
Beat him soft like clay
And stuffed him down the belly
Of a waiting jeep.
       What business of mine is it
       So long they don't take the yam
       From my savouring mouth?

They came one night
Booted the whole house awake
And dragged Danladi out,
Then off to a lengthy absence.
       What business of mine is it
       So long they don't take the yam
       From my savouring mouth?

Chinwe went to work one day
Only to find her job was gone:
No query, no warning, no probe –
Just one neat sack for a stainless record.
       What business of mine is it
       So long they don't take the yam
       From my savouring mouth?
And then one evening
As I sat down to eat my yam
A knock on the door froze my hungry hand
The jeep was waiting on my bewildered lawn
Waiting, waiting in its usual silence.

*Niyi Osundare*

Beaten to a pulp and like the earth

Links with previous image; belly soft like clay. Does he return?

Refrain – increasing irony, ridiculing the 'head in the sand attitude'

She had done no wrong

What price had he paid? His silence = food? Now he's hungry.

Doesn't understand why

### Niyi Osundare
Nigerian born in 1947. He says that there is no choice – the African poet must be political. "You cannot keep quiet about the situation in the kind of countries we find ourselves in, in Africa." In his poems he "holds mirrors in which his readers may see themselves in close up".

## HOW TO PLAN YOUR RESPONSE

| Points | Evidence | |
|---|---|---|
| Similarities | Vultures | Not My Business |
| • Both Nigerian poets | Chinua Achebe | Nivi Osundare |
| • Set in Africa – but issues apply in lots of countries | 'a vulture perching high' | Food = yam and people's names – Akanni, Danladi |
| • Protest against violence human beings inflict on others | Strong contrast of Belsen Commandant buying chocolate having spent the day killing innocent people in concentration camps during World War 2: 'fumes of human roast' | Image of beatings: 'beat him soft like clay/and stuffed him down' |
| • Poems about evil political regimes<br><br>• Names = personal | World War 2 Nazi Germany<br><br>Commandant of Belsen | 'they' – Africa – but could be other countries too<br><br>Victims Akanni, Danladi |
| • Protest against corrupt human instincts | 'Kindred love'<br>'perpetuity of evil' | 'don't take the yam from my savouring mouth' (cowardly) |
| • Protest against people who ignore what is happening to others and can't see evil | Image – 'charnel-house' and 'fall asleep – her face turned to the wall' | 'What business is it of mine'<br>'hungry hand'<br>silence, waiting jeep |
| • Feeding off others to survive | 'eyes of a swollen corpse'<br>'ate things in its bowel' | 'savouring mouth' |
| Differences | | |
| • Poetic voice | Impersonal third-person narration: 'his smooth bashed-in head' | Personal first-person narration: 'I sat down to eat my yam' |
| • Structure | Free verse – three sections (not stanzas), quite long | Regular pattern of stanzas and use of repeated chorus, quite short |
| • Setting | Moves from unnamed African landscape to named European place – Belsen | 'yam' gives only clue to unnamed African setting |
| • Language | Use of powerful words to create an impact: 'dawn unstirred by harbingers of sunbreak' 'icy caverns of a cruel heart' | Straightforward, matter-of-fact, sometimes casual language: 'They picked Akanni up one morning' |
| • Vocabulary | Wide range of difficult words used: 'harbinger', 'despondent', 'encapsulated', 'perpetuity' | Apart from African names, language is pretty straightforward, sometimes slang: 'stuffed', 'booted' |
| • Use of metaphor | Vultures representing human beings | No figurative language features |

# HOW TO WRITE A RESPONSE TO THE QUESTION

**Examiner comments**

A neat way to begin is to introduce the chosen poem and indicate an understanding of the task.

The poem I have chosen for comparison is 'Not My Business'. Like 'Vultures', it is written by a Nigerian poet and set in Africa. However, in both cases the African setting simply provides a background for events that could take place in many other countries around the world. Both poems protest about the way in which human beings treat each other, but they do so in different ways, using different techniques such as structure, vocabulary and poetic voice.

Personal comments indicate a good understanding, but beware of becoming too involved in the topic and your reactions to them.
Good use of quotations woven into the body of the writing. The last point is a good one.

The protest made in these poems makes me wonder why humans behave in the way that they do. How can the Commandant in Achebe's poem go shopping for chocolate with the smell of 'human roast' still 'clinging rebelliously to his hairy nostrils'? This horrifying image makes me feel the protest strongly. In a similar way, Osundare, when he writes about 'they' – the violent people who casually pick up Akanni one morning – makes me react strongly to the words 'beat him soft like clay'. The fact that the Belsen Commandant is identified in one poem and in the other the victim has a name, helps reinforce the protest because it becomes personal and specific.

Interesting points – these examples could equally have been used as differences as they are not quite the same thing.

Both poems also protest against the basic survival instincts of human beings, showing how they can be cowardly and corrupt. Achebe's poem tells the reader to 'despair' because 'Kindred love', love of family, can be infected with the 'germ' allowing 'the perpetuity of evil'. Similarly, Osundare thinks that eating just to survive can become a weak and cowardly act, as his poem suggests that there are people who will let anything happen to others, 'so long as they don't take the yam'.

First point is very good – shows a clear understanding of the message in both poems.
A clever way to link the two poems.
Not sure the last part has been fully understood.

Perhaps the strongest protest that comes through both poems is against those who turn a blind eye to the corrupt regimes that human beings create and allow to exist. This is the main focus of 'Not My Business', where the chorus is used ironically in the first three stanzas, 'What business is it of mine'. (This is absent from the last, leaving a 'hungry hand' and the 'silence'.) Achebe's vultures may well be feeding off victims from such a government, but his poem also creates a powerful image that asks how a woman in a 'charnel-house' can 'fall asleep – her face turned to the wall' ignoring all the horror around her.

# READING: POETRY

> *Very good points about Achebe. Perhaps more could have been said about Osundare's contrasting style.*

Achebe's use of powerful imagery is one of the main differences between the two poems. We have a clear vision of the vultures on their 'broken bone of a dead tree', with their 'dump of gross feathers'. His language creates an impact with words such as 'harbinger' and 'encapsulated', and metaphors such as 'icy caverns of a cruel heart', which are effective but challenging. In contrast, Osundare's language is straightforward and matter-of-fact – ensuring anyone can understand what he has to say.

> *Good to see a candidate tackling structure in this way and discussing the voices of the poems. Used the information well here to show how these features work.*

The two poems look very different on the page. Osundare's poem has a regular pattern and a clear structure using stanzas and a repeated chorus, whereas Achebe writes in a free verse, keeping his lines short, with no stanzas. There are also contrasting voices in these poems. 'Vultures' is written in the third person, with a narrator who observes and asks thought-provoking questions, whereas 'Not My Business' uses the first person to create a link between poet and reader. Both are effective ways of making a protest felt – in the first the reader is made to see the horror and answer the questions raised, in the second the reader becomes the guilty one, it is 'my savouring mouth' and 'my hungry hand'.

> *Rather short. One or two of these points should be supported.*

These poets have made their protest strongly felt through the language, imagery and structure they have used in their poems. Their voices are striking and their message is clear. I have learned a great deal from reading them.

## Overall comment

This response would gain a good grade because it examines both poems in **equal depth**, using appropriate references and quotations. Points are interesting, clearly expressed and well organised. The student has reacted to both poems **analytically** and **personally**.

 To test yourself, go to Reading: Comparing poems: Improving your answer.

60

# HOW TO APPROACH A WRITING QUESTION

- GCSE writing tasks will direct you towards a particular type of writing, for example to explain or persuade, to advise or inform.

- Your response will be assessed on how well it matches the criteria for that type of writing.

- In addition, you will gain credit for writing that is well-organised, uses interesting sentence structures and is accurate in terms of punctuation and spelling.

- The next eight units will help you to revise the key features for the main writing types in the exam.

## HOW TO READ THE TEXT ACTIVELY

The box below contains the introduction to a typical GCSE writing section. Read it through carefully to make sure you understand it.

At GCSE you are usually given a choice of two or three tasks. Make sure you **only answer one**.

Second part of the paper – following a reading section

This tells you the type of writing that is required

Following the **time** guidance is **very important**

### SECTION B: WRITING TO ARGUE, PERSUADE OR ADVISE

Sometimes there is a link between the theme or type of writing in the reading section and the tasks in the writing section

Answer **one** question in this section.
Spend about **45 minutes** on this section.
You may wish to link your response to information given in the reading section of the paper, but you do not have to do so.
If you use any information **do not simply copy it**.

This is very important – **never simply copy anything in an exam!** If you wish, use short quotations enclosed by inverted commas and make sure they are acknowledged.

**Planning is essential** to help you organise a good response. This is time well spent – but don't overdo it!

Remember:
- Spend five minutes **planning and organising** your response.
- You should write about **two sides of A4**, no more.
- Spend five minutes **checking** your paragraphing punctuation and spelling.

A **concise**, **quality** response is better than a long-winded, rambling one

Always leave time to **read through what you have written** – checking and correcting, and getting rid of repeated words are all essential for a quality piece of writing

## HOW TO SELECT A TASK

Once you have understood the instructions, it is time to make your choice and select a question.

Read through the choices available as there may be one to four options. For each one examine:

1 **the perspective** from which you are being asked to write – for example: as yourself, as someone representing a particular point of view, or as someone with a particular role within a named group.

2 **the form of writing** – for example a letter, a speech, an article for a newspaper or magazine, or an information leaflet.

3 **the purpose of the writing** – is it intended to: persuade, describe, explain, analyse, review, advise?

4 **the intended reader** – for whom is the writing intended? For example, people who have the power to make decisions, people your own age, children in need of information or advice, or adults with similar interests.

5 **the topic** you are being asked to write about – this may be something you know about or not, something you are interested in or not. Although the topic is important, remember it is not necessarily the most important thing. You may often be asked to write about a subject that does not really concern you particularly.

> **Remember!**
> - Make sure that your choice is not based on topic alone.
> - Consider which type of writing you can do best. If you can't write speeches, then choose something else, even if the topic appeals to you.
> - Choose a task that suits your style. Think about the level of formality or informality that the writing requires.

**Here are some typical examples of GCSE writing questions:**

1 **Perspective** from which you are being asked to write

2 **Form** that your writing will need to take

3 **Purpose** of the writing

4 **Intended readers**

5 **Topic** that the writing will be concerned with

**EITHER**

3. You are a student representative on the school council, which has been considering whether the school uniform should be changed. You have been asked to write a paper to be given to the headteacher **arguing** the case **against** a change.

*(27 marks)*

**OR**

4. Write a speech to be given at a local council meeting **persuading** the members to consider adopting a recycling programme for cans, bottles and paper as part of the refuse collection service.

*(27 marks)*

**OR**

5. Write an article for the **advice** column of a teenage magazine about the best ways to avoid stress during the three months before taking your GCSE exams.

*(27 marks)*

## HOW TO MAKE THE BEST USE OF YOUR TIME

Good timing is an essential part of success, but don't panic! Once you start the writing section of your GCSE examination, you need to know exactly how long to spend on each aspect of preparing, writing and checking your response.

Knowing how to divide your time beforehand will save time when it really matters, so be prepared.

These time guidelines are for a **45-minute task**, but you can adapt them to suit the needs of your particular exam requirements.

**Check how long you have before you start to plan your time.**

> **Remember!**
> • Make sure you have clearly written the section and question number you have answered at the beginning of your response.

### Part 1 - up to two minutes
- **Read through all the questions** carefully.
- **Select your task.**
- **Highlight the key words** of the task in terms of the five points on page 62.
- **Remind yourself of the key features** of the type of writing you have chosen.

### Part 2 - up to four minutes
- **Brainstorm your ideas on your chosen topic/task**, including points that you could cover and things you should include.
- **Select key ideas** from your brainstorm (use a highlighter), bearing your reader in mind.
- **Make a plan** from your selection, structuring your points in a logical and effective order.

### Part 3 - up to 29 minutes
- **Start to write**, covering about two sides of A4.
- **Use any presentational/layout features**, such as bullet points or headings, that you think are appropriate.
- **Be aware of the time limit** and make sure that you conclude your writing before your time runs out!

### Part 4 - up to five minutes
- **Read through** what you have written.
- **Check** your work, correcting **punctuation**, including **paragraph breaks**, changing **repeated/overused/dull words** by adding more interesting ones, and, of course, checking **spelling**.

 To test yourself, go to Writing: Approaching writing questions.

# HOW TO STRUCTURE YOUR WRITING

- Organising your writing well is essential if you wish to gain a good grade.

- Marks are specifically awarded for organisation, sentence structure and punctuation.

## HOW DO I KNOW IF MY WRITING IS WELL STRUCTURED?

As a quick reference, this chart shows what is expected of writing at grade C and above in terms of structure and organisation.

| Paragraphs should: | Sentences should: | Punctuation should: |
|---|---|---|
| ✔ be sequenced in a logical order<br>✔ indicate a change in focus<br>✔ have ideas organised within them<br>✔ be linked to one another in a coherent way. | ✔ include an appropriate mix of simple, compound and complex<br>✔ match purpose, form and intended reader<br>✔ use a range of different constructions<br>✔ be used to create an effect. | ✔ be generally accurate<br>✔ include a range appropriate to the purpose and form of the writing<br>✔ make meaning clear<br>✔ enhance the organisation of ideas. |

**Planning** your answer before you start is an essential part of creating a sound structure on which to base your writing. Planning provides you with a route or map, helping you to get safely from the beginning to the end of what you want to say in the given time – without getting lost in the middle!

Your writing should have at least **four** paragraphs, if not more, including:

- an introduction

- two middle paragraphs

- a conclusion.

## HOW TO CREATE INTERESTING SENTENCES

- Change the word order so that you start with a verb or an adverb, e.g. **Thoughtlessly, we often throw away things other people could use** or **Collecting cans for recycling in a school canteen is an obvious solution**.

- Put the subordinate clause first, e.g. **If the council agrees, this could be done at little extra cost**.

- Use one word as a sentence to create an emphasis or special effect, e.g. **Simple**.

### KEY ⚬━━━ CONCEPTS

**Structure: the order in which ideas are organised and arranged in a piece of writing.**

**Paragraph: a section of a piece of writing used to organise the ideas. A new paragraph should mark a new topic or change in focus and should guide the reader.**

**Complex sentence: a sentence that contains a main clause and one or more subordinate clauses, e.g.** When the rain started, everyone ran for shelter.

**Compound sentence: a sentence that has two or more main clauses, sometimes joined by a conjunction, e.g.** Ayisha wanted to go for a walk but Lucy preferred to stay inside and watch TV.

## HOW TO WRITE A GOOD INTRODUCTION

- Your first sentence and the rest of the introductory paragraph are very important because they are the first thing that the reader, including an examiner, reads.

- They need to set the tone for what is to follow, and consequently you must make sure that they catch the reader's interest in an appropriate way – one that suits the purpose and form of the writing.

### A good opening sentence:

✔ makes a clear link with the given topic or theme

✔ adopts the appropriate tone for the type of writing

✔ engages the reader's interest

✔ doesn't begin, 'In this essay I am going to…'.

### A good introduction:

✔ is concise, clear and to the point

✔ indicates the main topics to be considered

✔ doesn't go into lots of specific details or examples

✔ leads the reader naturally into the rest of the writing.

The following are examples of an effective opening sentence and introduction in response to question 4 from page 62.

> Have you ever thought about what happens to the contents of the large black bag that is mysteriously whisked away from your dustbin every Tuesday morning?

This is a successful **opening sentence** because it:

- addresses the reader directly

- gives the reader something to think about

- introduces the topic that is to follow in an imaginative way.

### Opening paragraph

*Creates an image in the reader's mind*

*Introduces a suggestion of fear*

*Use of first person links the reader and the writer together*

*Makes the topic sound important and urgent*

*Imaginative use of vocabulary*

*Impressive phrase*

> Imagine a world where once-green fields are covered in piles of smouldering rubbish and the price of a can of cola is beyond the reach of the average person. It may sound like science fiction, but this could be our world by the time I'm 25. We need to introduce a recycling programme that works now – before it is too late. These are some of my suggestions to prevent the burial of our world and the squandering of the world's finite natural resources.

*Provides a lead in to the rest of the speech and the topics to be covered*

**Why this is an effective opening paragraph:**

- It is interesting and concise.

- It links the reader to the topic imaginatively to begin with, becoming more practical at the end.

## HOW TO MAINTAIN THE READER'S INTEREST

Having a strong introduction is important, but make sure that the rest of your writing retains the same style. Once you have gained the reader's attention, you need to keep hold of it.

Effective ways to do this include:

- using a **wide** and **interesting vocabulary**
- using a variety of **different sentence structures**
- varying sentence length to create an effect
- making interesting and **thoughtful points**
- introducing a **dash of humour** where appropriate.

The following example is a paragraph from the middle part of a response to the same question.

### Hints

- Use topic sentences to guide your reader's attention at the beginning of a paragraph.
- Organise points within paragraphs so they fit together well.
- Make sure your paragraphs follow logically on from one to another.

---

*Topic sentence introduces the paragraph*

*Good use of link words*

*Using a question helps to maintain interest – it is a persuasive tactic*

*Final, balanced sentence draws the paragraph neatly to its conclusion*

*Link word used to connect the two paragraphs*

One of my suggestions concerns the recycling of glass. Currently many people regularly take their bottles to the local bottle bank in the supermarket car park. Although this is a start, it can cause problems for some people. For example, those who walk to the supermarket, or go by bus, are reluctant to carry heavy, dangerous and rattling bottles. These already 'eco-friendly' members of the public have no option but to throw away their glass with their ordinary rubbish – a risky business. Wouldn't it be better if bottles were collected from our homes? This would not only be safer and easier for people, it would also ensure that a higher percentage would be recycled.

Another recycling issue concerns paper. While newspapers are collected in some places, other paper and cardboard products, such as food packaging and magazine, have to be thrown away...

*Sentence begins in a less conventional way*

*Quotation marks and a dash introduce a wider variety of punctuation*

*Short sentence creates a greater impact*

### Why this is an effective paragraph:

- It is logically constructed, carefully moving from the introduction of a topic, to an exploration of points, finally suggesting a solution in the conclusion.
- It uses a variety of different sentence constructions.
- It maintains the reader's interest through the introduction of thoughtful ideas.
- It is written in appropriate style for its purpose.

# HOW TO WRITE A STRONG CONCLUSION

A strong conclusion is essential as it helps to round off your writing and draw your ideas together for the reader's final attention. It is also one of the most difficult parts of your writing as, at this stage, you are probably running short of time and feel you have said everything that you want to say.

A good conclusion will:

- remind readers of the **purpose** of the writing
- make a **link** with the introduction
- **highlight** a few main points that have already been considered
- be **concise**
- provide a **definite ending**.

Here is an example of a conclusion to the recycling speech.

┌─ Concluding words ─┐
as a final point
lastly
finally
ultimately
to conclude
in conclusion
to finish
in the end
consequently
as you can see
as I have shown

---

*Signals a conclusion*

*Reminds readers of the purpose of the writing*

*Link with introduction*

*Draws ideas together*

> Finally, I am sure you will agree that my suggestions will indeed help to reduce waste and encourage people to recycle more of their so-called 'rubbish'. As I said earlier, it isn't really rubbish at all, but simply another part of the process of making new products for the hungry shopping 'demon'. If we want a future where we can still sit reading a magazine in a green field, sipping a cool drink from a handy, clean can, we will have to organise ourselves and take greater responsibility for the waste products that result from our lifestyle. Surely collecting empty bottles and clear plastic bags from our doorsteps isn't too heavy a price to pay? It doesn't cost the earth to save the earth.

*Introduces a point made previously*

*A definite concluding sentence, giving a strong final message*

**Why this is an effective conclusion:**

- It is carefully constructed.
- It is to the point and concise.
- It is persuasive – which was the given purpose of the writing.
- It uses imaginative imagery.
- It maintains the interest of the reader.

---

To test yourself, go to Writing – Structuring your writing.

# WRITING TO INFORM

**Key features of information writing**

**Intended reader:** someone who wants **know** about something.
**Purpose:** to provide information that is **clear and easily understood**.
**Structure:** **logical**, **non-chronological**, sometimes organised in terms of categories with sub-headings.
**Language features:** writing should:

- use a **formal tone**
- be **concise** and to the point
- focus on **facts** and details related to the subject
- be written in the **present tense** (unless it concerns an event that has already taken place)
- **impersonal** – written in the **third person** (unless directed otherwise)
- depending on the form of writing (e.g. a leaflet), it may use **layout conventions** that help the reader to access information easily such as headings and bullet points.

**Intended readers**

**Form** that your writing will take

Following your examinations in July, your school has been invited to take part in an exchange scheme with 16-year-old students from Canada. You have been asked to write a contribution to the 'Visitors' Information Pack' they will be sent, outlining important facts about living in your town that you think will help to prepare them for their visit.

**Write an informative article about your town.**

**Spend about 45 minutes on this section.**

**Perspective –** from which you will be writing

**Purpose –** why you are writing

**Topic** that will be the focus of your writing

## HOW TO START ANSWERING A QUESTION LIKE THIS

- ✔ **Remind yourself of the key features** of informative writing.
- ✔ **Use a spider diagram to gather your ideas**, including several points you could cover.
- ✔ **Select**, by highlighting, the main points you wish to include.
- ✔ **Plan** from your selection, putting the points in a logical order.

## HOW TO GATHER YOUR IDEAS USING A SPIDER DIAGRAM

- **Space your ideas** over the page so you can add wide range.
- **Highlight** the best/most important ideas of things you'd like to include.
- **Number** your potential paragraphs in a logical order.

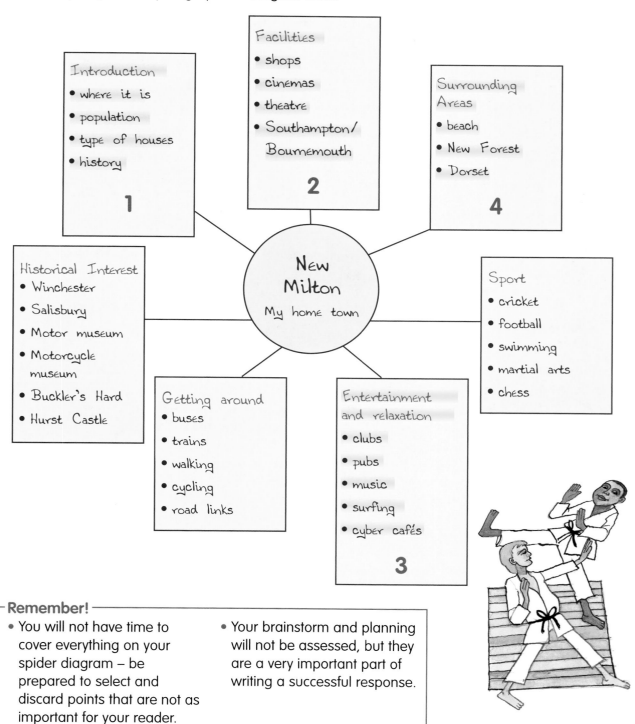

**Remember!**

- You will not have time to cover everything on your spider diagram – be prepared to select and discard points that are not as important for your reader.

- Your brainstorm and planning will not be assessed, but they are a very important part of writing a successful response.

## HOW TO TURN A PLAN INTO A RESPONSE

- Once you have gathered your ideas, you need to **select** those that are most important to your reader.

- Draw up **a brief plan** that you can refer to whilst you are writing.

*Each number represents a new paragraph*

*Logical order moves from essential practical information through to entertainment*

| Plan - structure |
|---|
| 1. Introduction: where New Milton is, etc. |
| 2. Facilities, e.g. shops |
| 3. Entertainment and relaxation |
| 4. Surrounding areas |
| 5. Conclusion - where to find more info (e.g. website) |

## WRITING AN INTRODUCTION

When starting to write an information text:

- give your writing a **heading** obviously linked with the topic

- clearly establish the topic in your **opening sentence**

- observe the **language features** associated with this type of writing.

Here is an example of a well-written introductory paragraph:

*Establishes topic clearly and immediately*

*Main heading indicates subject*

*Present tense*

*Formal tone*

*Factual*

*Final sentence bringing the first paragraph to a conclusion and introducing others that will follow*

*Paragraph covers points from point 1 on plan and spider diagram*

> Welcome to New Milton
>
> New Milton is a couple of miles from the south coast in Hampshire, between the New Forest and the sea. About 23,000 people live in and around the town, which means that it is quite a small place. Although a village called Milton has been here for many centuries, New Milton really started developing as a town about a hundred years ago, when the railway arrived. Some of the shops on the High Street were built then, though they are now quite up-to-date. A few buildings are much older, but many of the houses were built in the 1960s; some are still being built on the edges of the town today. Overall it is a pretty typical, small English town, with all the usual amenities, surrounded by interesting places that are easy to visit.

## HOW TO CONTINUE AND COMPLETE YOUR INFORMATION WRITING

To test yourself, go to Writing – Writing to inform.

Once you have written the introduction, continue your writing by following the points outlined in your plan. As you do so make sure that you:

• keep to the **point**

• maintain all the **language features** that are part of writing to inform

• bring your writing to a **conclusion** within the time limit.

Here are some examples taken from further paragraphs:

---

*Sub-heading helps to guide the reader*

*This second paragraph covers point 2 on the original plan*

> Shops and facilities
>
> There are so many shops along the high street, almost anything can be bought in New Milton. However, it is best to head into nearby Southampton, which has an amazing new shopping centre, for up-to-the-minute CDs and clothes. This is also the best place to go to see newly-released films...

*Indicates an awareness of the reader's interest as they are teenagers*

---

*Covers point 3 on the plan*

> Entertainment and relaxation
>
> New Milton is not exactly a 'hot spot' for clubs, but the nearby city of Bournemouth is a great place to go for a bit of fun and excitement in the evening. During the day...

*Expression aimed at intended reader*

---

*Useful summing up phrase*

> ...As can be seen, anyone interested in history or outdoor activities will have plenty to see and do, during a stay in New Milton as there are so many things to do.

*Covers point 4 on the plan*

---

*Covers point 5 on the plan*

> ...This is just a brief introduction to the town of New Milton and what it has to offer the visitor. More information is available on the many websites linked with the town and the New Forest.

*Useful way to end – directs reader to somewhere else they can find what they need to know*

---

**Why this is a good response**

• It is clearly focused on the given task and is logically structured.

• It follows the conventions expected of information writing by maintaining the use of the present tense and third person.

• Expression is mostly formal, but occasionally more casual words and phrases are used to create interest for the intended reader.

• This awareness of reader and purpose is also reflected in the selection of information.

# WRITING TO EXPLAIN

┌─ **Key features of writing to explain** ─────────

**Intended reader:** usually someone who wants to **understand** a point of view, a course of action, a process or rationale.

**Purpose:** to provide answers to a question, give reasons, or help someone understand a process.

**Structure:** **logical** step-by-step points.

**Language features** – When writing to explain you should:

- use **general statements** to introduce the subject at the beginning
- be written in a **formal style**
- be unemotional and adopt an **impersonal tone** (even when dealing with a personal subject)
- use the **present tense**
- use causal connectives such as **since**, **because**, **therefore**
- use **complex sentences**
- contain **technical vocabulary**, where appropriate to the topic.

└──────────────────────────────────────────────

**Intended readers**

**Topic**

**Purpose**

**Perspective** or personal point of view

**Form** part of a booklet

The Head of Year 10 has asked you to write a contribution to a Year 9 into Year 10 booklet explaining which of your GCSE subjects you think has been most beneficial.

Write your contribution, *explaining* the benefits of the subject you have chosen

Spend about 45 minutes on this section.

## HOW TO START ANSWERING A QUESTION LIKE THIS

✔ Look really carefully at what the question is asking you to do. What is the purpose of the writing? Who is the audience? What is the perspective from which you must write?

✔ Choose your **subject** with care. Focus on the word 'beneficial' – it is not asking about your favourite subject but the one that is the **most useful**.

✔ Remind yourself of the **key features of writing to explain**.

## HOW TO PLAN EXPLANATION WRITING

Being **logical** and **clear** are important when writing an explanation that your reader will understand. In your planning, think of the points you wish to make as a series of connected circles, one leading on from the other. For example:

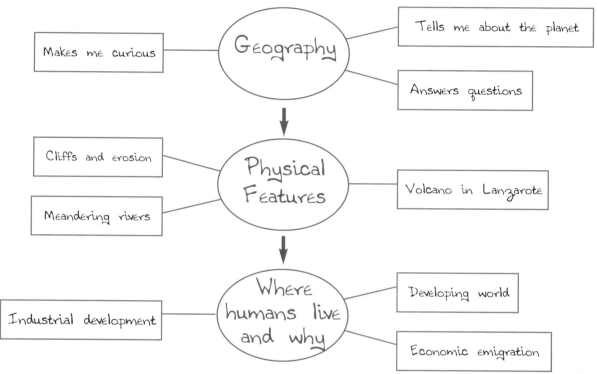

Makes me curious — Geography — Tells me about the planet / Answers questions

Cliffs and erosion / Meandering rivers — Physical Features — Volcano in Lanzarote

Industrial development — Where humans live and why — Developing world / Economic emigration

## IMPORTANT VOCABULARY

- You need to show **links** between the ideas you are explaining. Useful link words and phrases include: **in order to, then, next, when, as a result, since.**

- You may sometimes need **technical vocabulary**. Make sure it can be easily understood by the reader, especially if your audience is young people.

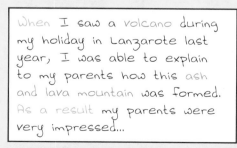

When I saw a volcano during my holiday in Lanzarote last year, I was able to explain to my parents how this ash and lava mountain was formed. As a result my parents were very impressed...

**Key**

———— Link words

———— Technical vocabulary

## WRITING AN INTRODUCTION

In your **introduction**, you will need to:

- catch the attention of your reader
- focus on the topic given in the task
- give a brief outline of some of your main points
- give reasons to support your points
- maintain the reader's interest so they will want to read on.

Here is an example of an introduction and following paragraphs:

*Interesting, bold statement catches the reader's attention*

*Introduces some general points that can be explained later*

*2nd paragraph is a logical development following a point made in the introduction*

*Explanation following link word, reminding the reader of the topic*

*Clear focus on the topic set*

*Link word*

*Complex sentence*

*Formal style*

*Explanation following link word*

Learning about our planet and its people is fascinating. That is why the most useful subject I have studied during my GCSE course is geography. I find this subject fascinating, because it makes me curious about places and the landscape around me, then it provides me with the answers.

Geography helps me to enjoy the natural, physical features of our planet. Now I can walk along a beach and understand why the cliffs above me are crumbling. When I saw a volcano during my holiday in Lanzarote last year, I was able to explain to my parents how this ash and lava mountain was formed. My parents were very impressed but, more importantly, I felt more in touch with the place I was visiting and had a better understanding of the island.

Since I started studying geography, I understand more about the development of industry in Sunderland, where I was born. In fact, it enables me to learn more about people and countries around the world. This is beneficial because people from many different nationalities live in my community and I think geography helps people to have a better understanding of one another...

# HOW TO BRING YOUR EXPLANATION TO A CONCLUSION

In your **conclusion**:

1. remind your reader of the reason for writing

2. give a brief summary of your main points

3. end with a clear, positive statement.

*1. Remind your reader of the reason for writing*

During your time in Years 10 and 11, you will study a variety of subjects and learn many new and interesting details about living in the world around you. As you can see, for me the most useful of these subjects has been geography. It is a subject that offers great variety in terms of all the topics that it covers, from the physical features of our planet to the development of industry in our own country and around the world. Through studying geography I have gained a better understanding of how the world was made, its people and the way it works. This will doubtless be very helpful to me no matter what I choose to do in the future, because no matter what I do or where I go I will be working on this planet with its people and industries. Geography has given me a clearer vision through my window on the world.

*2. Give a brief summary of the points you have made*

*3. End with a clear, positive statement*

## Why this is a good response

- The opening paragraph is concise and creates interest. It introduces some explanations to be explored later.

- The writer uses a formal tone, even though the task demands a personal perspective for a teenage audience.

- A variety of sentence types, including some complex sentences, maintain the reader's interest.

- Clear explanations have been given, helping the reader to understand the writer's point of view.

- There is a strong conclusion drawing together points made and reminding the reader of the benefits of the subject chosen.

To test yourself, go to Writing – Writing to explain.

# WRITING TO DESCRIBE

## Key features of descriptive writing

**Intended reader:** will vary according to the nature of the task – it could be a **personal** record (e.g. a diary) or **for others**.

**Purpose:** to communicate a **feeling** or **experience**, to create a **visual image** portraying a place, person, action or object, to create **an effect**.

**Structure:** mostly **non-chronological** (depending on the task); usually logical.

**Language features** – when writing to describe you should:

- use adjectives and adverbs
- use powerful verbs and nouns
- often make comparisons using **figurative language**, such as similes, metaphors and personification
- write from a **personal** perspective, including feelings.
- use the past, present or sometimes even the future tense
- be **imaginative** or **factual**.

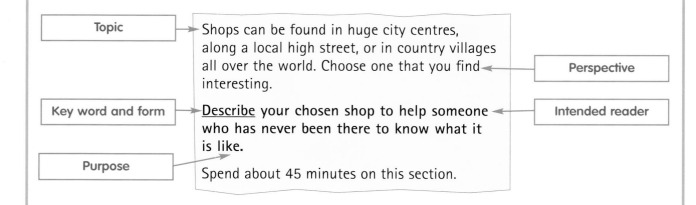

**Topic**

Shops can be found in huge city centres, along a local high street, or in country villages all over the world. Choose one that you find interesting.

**Perspective**

**Key word and form**

<u>Describe</u> your chosen shop to help someone who has never been there to know what it is like.

**Intended reader**

**Purpose**

Spend about 45 minutes on this section.

## HOW TO ANSWER A QUESTION LIKE THIS

✔ **Choose** a shop that you know well – one that is interesting and has enough features that could be described.

✔ **Brainstorm your observations** about the shop (see the example on page 77) try to see it in your mind's eye.

✔ Remind yourself of the **key features of descriptive writing** and how they link with the task.

✔ **Select ideas and plan your writing** – think about how to organise the features you are going to describe. Will you start with the outside and then move in, or begin inside and only use this as your focus?

## WHAT THE EXAMINERS ARE LOOKING FOR

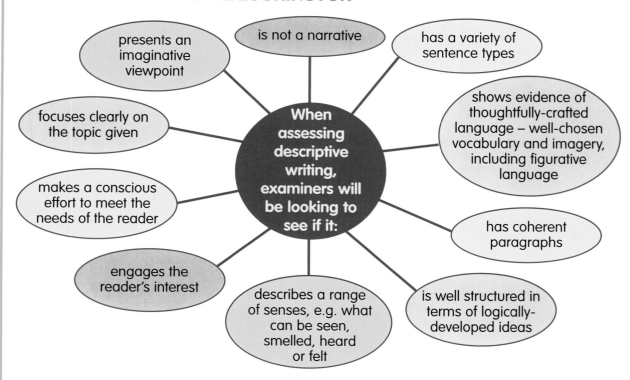

## HOW TO WRITE AN EFFECTIVE DESCRIPTION

### Make use of powerful verbs, adverbs and adjectives

- These descriptive words are central building blocks in helping to make your writing vivid and evocative.

  Powerful verbs will help to improve your descriptive writing. The following sentence is fine, but the verbs could be more imaginative:

  *The lights hanging from the ceiling shine, lighting up the room.*

- A more interesting effect is achieved simply by changing the verbs:

  *The lights suspended from the ceiling flicker, illuminating the room.*

- Adding adverbs gives the reader more information, giving them a clearer picture:

  *The lights suspended precariously from the ceiling flicker faintly, illuminating the room.*

- Finally, adjectives create a greater impact:

  *The lights suspended precariously from the dusty ceiling, flicker faintly, illuminating the gloomy room.*

# WRITING

## Remember!

- It is important not to overuse figurative language in your writing – it could become rather like eating too much chocolate cake.

## Make comparisons

- You can compare one thing with another through figurative language. There are several ways to do this.
- At the simplest level, you could use a simile. This type of comparison helps to create a picture in your reader's mind. For example:

  *There are rows of untidy books standing on the shelves.*

  becomes much more interesting with the addition of a simile:

  *The rows of untidy books on the shelves stand like worn and weary soldiers after a long march.*

- A metaphor is a more complex form of comparison and creates a stronger image in the mind of the reader. For example:

  *The old black till has levers that creak when they are pressed.*

  could be turned into:

  *At the press of a lever the till, a black-cloaked malevolent wizard, whirls into creaking action.*

- Personification is another way to bring descriptive writing imaginatively into life, by giving inanimate objects human feelings and movements. For example:

  *In a dusty corner of the room there are heaps of ancient magazines.*

  could become:

  *Ashamed, heaps of ancient magazines hide themselves, creeping forlornly into a dusty, forgotten corner of the room.*

## HOW TO WRITE A RESPONSE TO THE QUESTION

Here is an example of part of a response to the task given on page 76. It goes a long way towards meeting the assessment criteria given opposite.

In a tiny village on the far western coast of South Wales, there is a book shop that fascinates me. From the outside, 'Ivor's – Special Books for Little People', as its copperplate sign announces, is a very dishevelled building. It is the last in a row of terraced houses along the main street. What must once have been cheerful, sunny, yellow walls are now dull and faded. Cracks and mould spring from its dark corners giving it the appearance of a grumpy, frowning old man.

Entering, especially on a bright, sunny day, is like stepping into the gloomy cavern of a troll. The musty smelling dampness envelopes those who dare to tramp along its maze of narrow corridors, until at last the book-infested chamber is discovered. The lights suspended precariously from the dusty ceiling, flicker faintly, illuminating the gloomy room.

The rows of untidy books on the shelves stand like worn and weary soldiers after a long march. They are all children's books from long lost childhoods. Ashamed, heaps of ancient magazines hide themselves, creeping forlornly into a dusty, forgotten corner of the room. 'Boys' Own', 'The Eagle', 'Girl' all sleep quietly now, their picture stories belonging to another age.

Here all is hushed as a church, until at last a selection, a purchase, is made. Reluctantly, Bronwyn, Ivor's 65-year-old-daughter, stirs 'to be of service'. At the press of a lever the till, a black-cloaked malevolent wizard, tings and whirls into creaking action. Magically as money is spirited away it snaps shut. Silence. Bliss.

**Annotations:**

- Introduces and focuses on the topic given
- Strong image
- Sense of smell
- Well structured – paragraphs follow logically
- Simile
- Personification
- One-word sentences create an effect
- What can be heard
- Imaginative viewpoint
- Alliteration creates interest for the reader

**Why this is a good response**

- It engages the reader's interest by giving descriptive detail that creates strong images. The reader gains a real feeling of the place described.

- The writer chooses words with care and with a view to crafting a deliberate effect. The use of figurative language adds to this impression.

- The writing is logically structured, using well-defined paragraphs and a variety of sentence types.

To test yourself, go to Writing – Writing to describe.

# WRITING TO PERSUADE

**Key features of writing to persuade**

**Intended reader:** someone you are trying to **convince** or **influence**.

**Purpose:** to **change** the way someone thinks; to **advertise** or market goods or services.

**Structure:** logical, non-chronological, usually a number of points supporting a **single viewpoint**.

**Language features** – when writing to persuade you should use:

- use the present tense
- use personal pronouns such as **your, my, ours, we**
- choose adjectives and adverbs to **influence** the reader
- use **figurative language** such as similes, metaphors, etc. where appropriate
- make use of **repetition**
- introduce **rhetorical questions**
- use **informal** expression where appropriate
- make use of **emotive** language (i.e. language that appeals to the emotions rather than the brain).

---

**Perspective** – from which you will be writing

**Form** that your writing will take

Your wealthy aunt has offered to take one of her many nieces or nephews with her on an adventure tour of Australia in August next year. She will choose the one who can give her the best reasons why they should go.

**Write a letter to your aunt persuading her that you should be the one to join her.**

Spend about 45 minutes on this section.

**Intended reader**

**Topic** that will be the focus of your writing

**Purpose** – why you are writing

## HOW TO START

✔ Think through the key features of **persuasive writing**.

✔ Remind yourself of the **conventions** concerned with writing **informal letters**.

✔ Make a **diagram** of the ideas and persuasive arguments you could use (see page 81).

✔ **Select**, by highlighting, the main points you want to use.

✔ **Plan** your letter from your selection, putting your points in a logical order.

## HOW TO PRODUCE A PIECE OF EFFECTIVE PERSUASIVE WRITING

Good persuasive writing uses a series of arguments to convince the reader. In planning your arguments, it is useful to think of them in terms of a 'three-pronged attack', which in the planning stage would look like this:

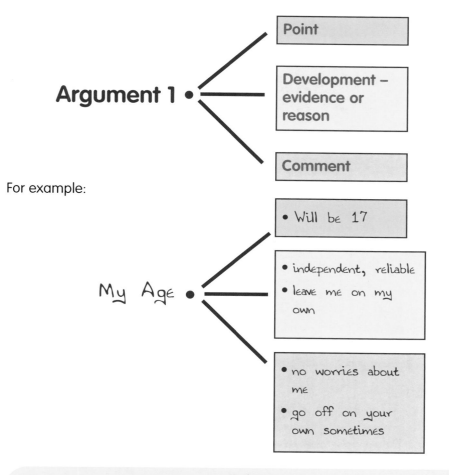

**Argument 1**
- Point
- Development – evidence or reason
- Comment

For example:

**My Age**
- Will be 17
- independent, reliable
- leave me on my own
- no worries about me
- go off on your own sometimes

**Remember!**
Use persuasive 'weasel' words and phrases – it is hard to argue against them:
- I am sure you'll agree...
- All I ask is...
- Everyone knows that...
- It is unlikely that...
- Only an idiot would think that...
- Intelligent people agree...
- People who care say that...

**Key**

Point

Development

Comment

Next year I will be a reliable 17-year-old, independent and capable of looking after myself. This means that you can be free from worrying about me. In fact you will confidently be able to leave me to my own devices sometimes, to give you an opportunity to have some time to yourself to visit an art gallery perhaps or go shopping on your own.

*Persuasive point*

*Persuasive advantage to the reader*

*Enticing the reader*

## HOW TO SET OUT AND WRITE AN INFORMAL LETTER

The letter the task is asking you to write is informal because your aunt is someone you know. In this case, you will put your address at the top of the letter.

This is how you should set out your letter:

*Your address*

*The date*

> 72 Union Street
> Ashbourne
> Derbyshire
> DE6 1FT
> 8 April 2004

*Greeting*

Dear Aunty Louie,

*Persuasive adjectives*

*Persuasive cliché*

How astonishingly kind of you to offer to take one of your devoted nephews or nieces with you on what sounds like a splendidly exciting trip across Australia. Of course, I know we would all like to go, but in all honesty I think you will find that I would be the one who could be of best service to you, helping to make your journey easier and more enjoyably entertaining.

*Second paragraph develops point introduced above into powerful argument*

Next year I will be a reliable 17-year-old, independent and capable of looking after myself. This means that you can be free from worrying about me. In fact, you will confidently be able to leave me to my own devices sometimes, to give you an opportunity to have some time to yourself to visit an art gallery perhaps or go shopping on your own.

*Rhetorical question – persuasively reminds the aunt of good times they have previously had together*

On the other hand, I am really looking forward to spending time with you on this trip. Being with you is always great fun. Remember the time when you took me for a trip on the 'London Eye' a few years ago? It was such an exciting adventure, although I have to admit to being a bit frightened beforehand. Your good humour soon dispelled all my doubts and we had a whale of a time together. I always value your big-hearted spirit and exuberance.

# WRITING

Of course, going to Australia together will be another great adventure we could share. You know it has always been a place that I have wanted to visit – ever since you showed me the kangaroos at Whipsnade Zoo, when I was six years old. Wildlife is another interest that we share. Won't it be wonderful for us to see all those amazing creatures in their natural habitat, together?

I am certain that you will need to consider the requests of all my cousins equally, alongside mine. Every one of us will have admirable reasons for wishing to join you on what promises to be the experience of a lifetime. All I ask is that you reflect on the enjoyable times we have shared together in the past. You must agree, we always get on so well, don't we? The attention and encouragement you have given me over the years has helped me to be more confident, as well as developing my own interests. For this I will always be grateful.

Now I would like to be given the opportunity to repay your kindness by helping you – as far as I am able – by being a friendly, considerate companion on your great adventure to the other side of the world. Whatever your decision, I will always be your adoring nephew.

Yours affectionately,

Luke

> *Use of personal pronouns emphasises the link between the reader and the writer*

> *Weasel phrases – it is difficult to argue against them*

> *Conclusion – a final persuasive reminder of a point made in the opening paragraph*

> *Appropriate ending – not too formal, conveying feeling*

> *Sign using the name the person knows you by – no surname!*

## Why this is a good response

- It is clearly organised and well structured.
- The content and style consistently matches the purpose and reader.
- There is evidence of quite a wide vocabulary and a range of sentence structures.

- Persuasive points are often subtle and are carefully introduced to influence the reader, showing a sound understanding of the principles of persuasive writing. For example, the emphasis is on how he can help his aunt, rather than focusing on his own wishes and desires.

- The conventions of an informal letter have been followed correctly.

 To test yourself, go to Writing – Writing to persuade.

# WRITING TO ARGUE

**Key features of argumentative writing**

**Intended reader:** someone who is interested in an **issue** or who needs to be convinced.

**Purpose:** to present a case for or against a point of view to **convince** the reader.

**Structure:** logically-developed paragraphs, making a series of **contrasting points**.

**Language features** – when writing to argue you should:

- use the present tense
- employ a **formal** tone
- use **logical connectives** such as **but, so, consequently, therefore, as a result**
- make it **impersonal** or **personal** depending on the nature of the topic and the task
- use **rhetorical questions**, if appropriate
- avoid personal or aggressive remarks.

**Topic** that will be the focus of your writing

**Form** that your writing will take

You are a student representative on the school council, which has been considering whether the school uniform should be changed. You have been chosen to write a letter to the headteacher, outlining the school council's reasons for not wanting to change the uniform.

Write a formal letter to the headteacher arguing the case against changing the school uniform.

Spend about 45 minutes on this section.

**Perspective** – from which you will be writing

**Intended reader**

**Purpose** – why you are writing

## HOW TO START

✔ Think about the key features of **argumentative writing**.

✔ Remind yourself of the **conventions** concerned with writing **formal letters**.

✔ Make a **diagram** of the reasons against changing the uniform that have been agreed by the school council

✔ **Select,** by highlighting, the main points you want to use.

✔ **Plan** your letter by putting your selected points into a logical order. For example, you could start with those that most concern the students, moving on to those that are more to do with the local community, leading up to a strong final point.

## HOW TO ARGUE A CASE EFFECTIVELY

Depending on the nature of the task, the strategy for good argumentative writing can be approached in two different ways:

1 You can focus entirely on **one point of view**, almost to the exclusion of any other. This approach uses many of the features and structure found in persuasive writing; for example, **point, evidence, comment** (see pages 28-31).

2 You can give a reasoned argument by **presenting different points of view,** both for and against. This approach anticipates the reader's possible counter arguments. By demonstrating why they should be dismissed, the case for the writer's point of view is strengthened. This type of argumentative writing uses the structure given below.

| ORDER | Against | | | For |
|---|---|---|---|---|
| 3 | Cost - very expensive | * | * | Using cheap suppliers |
| 2 | Wasteful - already have a uniform to wear | * | * | No real cost as teenagers outgrow clothes anyway |
| 5 | Like present uniform - modern and practical | * | * | New uniform more 'upmarket' |
| 4 | School identification in the community | * | * | A change in image is needed |
| 1 | Present one looks good - why change? | * | * | New blazers look impressive |

One way to construct an argument is to 'set it up and knock it down' – that is, begin with an opposing point and then show why it is unreasonable or incorrect by making your own point. Here is an example:

**Key**

| | |
|---|---|
| Counter argument in favour of a change | Writer's argument against a change |
| Reason for rejecting the counter argument | Establishing the writer's point of view |

It has been argued that teenagers grow so fast their clothes need to be changed frequently anyway, but I would say that this idea is an exaggeration. In addition, many students have only recently bought a new uniform in the last few weeks; this will not be outgrown until well into the next school year. Therefore, changing the uniform in September will cause a great deal of wastage and extra expense.

Remember!

**Set it up**
- It can be said that…
- It could be argued that…
- Many people think that…
- It has been suggested that…

**Knock it down**
- On the other hand…
- But…
- However…
- If you consider…
- Conversely…
- On the contrary…

## HOW TO SET OUT AND WRITE A FORMAL LETTER

The letter the task is asking you to write is **formal** because you are writing as a representative of the school council. In this case you will need to put two addresses at the top of the letter.

This is how you should set out your letter:

*Your address*

*The date*

*Name and address of person you are writing to*

12, Carlton Bank
Harpenden,
Herts
AL5 4UT

Mr A Conningham
Headteacher
Westwood School
Harpenden
Herts
AL5 5UY

12 January 2004

*Greeting*

Dear Mr Conningham,

*Clearly introduces the subject and purpose of the letter*

Following your request, the school council has been considering your proposal to change the school uniform next year. We have looked at several arguments and weighed up the pros and cons for each. Our conclusions are summarised below.

*Counter argument*
*– reasons for rejecting it*
*– writer's point of view*

Firstly, it has been suggested that the proposed new uniform will create a more impressive image for the school. However, we do not think that ties and blazers with the school crest will change anything. Are people really going to be impressed by out-of-date badges and clothes belonging to the previous century? Sweatshirts are modern, cheap, comfortable and easy to wash. We like our uniform as it is. Royal purple suits us; it is the only 'badge' we need.

*Logical development of a point raised in previous paragraph*

It has been argued that teenagers grow so fast their clothes need to be changed frequently anyway, but I would say that this idea is an exaggeration. In addition, many students have only recently bought a new uniform in the last few weeks; this will not be outgrown until well into the next school year. Therefore, changing the uniform in September will cause a great deal of wastage and extra expense.

Although it has been said that the school will try to cut down costs by using inexpensive suppliers for the new uniform, the school council were not convinced. We were told that the new blazers alone will cost about £35, and in addition there is the extra cost of ties and badges. This is simply too much for many families to pay – particularly those with two or more children attending the school. If you consider that the present school sweatshirt is only £15, it is easy to see why we think the new uniform is too expensive.

*Use of 'set them up and knock them down' phrases and technique*

It appears that the governors and teachers think that having a new uniform will help our school establish a better image, competing with the other schools in the area. The school council feels that, on the contrary, it will have a damaging effect. Westwood is a well-known and popular school in the town and the students are easily identified by their striking modern uniform. It marks us out from the crowd. If we change the uniform people will lose this connection. Won't we then just look like all the others?

*Use of rhetorical question to refute counter argument*

Finally, it has to be said that the students are not in favour of this more 'upmarket' expensive uniform. Blazers and ties are simply not our style; they are expensive, old-fashioned and impractical. Our present uniform is practical, modern and comfortable. We wear it proudly, because it represents us, our school and what we believe we are – a modern, up-to-date comprehensive school.

*Conclusion – a summary of the most important arguments, clearly stating the writer's point of view*

*Powerful final sentence*

Yours sincerely,

Sadiqa Ullah

Westwood School Council Member

*End with 'sincerely' when you know the person's name, otherwise end with 'faithfully'*

*Sign using your full name (and position where appropriate)*

## Why this is a good response

- The arguments used are logical and coherently structured.
- The content and style is suitably formal, showing appreciation of the purpose and reader.
- At times, quite a wide vocabulary and a range of sentence structures have been used, including rhetorical questions.

- Arguments and counter arguments have been given with a degree of confidence, demonstrating an understanding of how to convince the reader effectively.
- The conventions of a formal letter have been followed correctly.

 To test yourself, go to Writing – Writing to argue.

# WRITING TO ADVISE

**Key features of writing to advise**

**Intended reader:** someone who needs recommendations, opinions or suggestions.

**Purpose:** to give guidance.

**Structure:** logically developed paragraphs.

**Language features** – when writing advice you should:

- use a formal or informal tone depending on the **form** and **reader**
- generally use the **present tense**
- use **personal pronouns** so the writing is aimed directly at the reader
- balance **positive** and **negative** points
- maintain a balance between friendliness and authority, **informality** and **formality**
- make the ideas sound attractive and **easy to follow**
- don't be aggressive – you are not giving orders
- be **reasonable** – make it sound like something the reader would have thought out for themselves anyway.

**Perspective** – from which you will be writing

**Form** that your writing will take

**Topic** that will be the focus of your writing

You are a columnist on a popular teenage magazine.

Write a special feature article giving advice to your teenage readers about how to find a suitable summer job after taking their GCSE exams.

Spend about 45 minutes on this section.

**Purpose** – why you are writing

Intended readers

## HOW TO START

✔ Look carefully at the question, thinking about the **perspective**, **purpose**, **audience** and **form**.

✔ Review the features of **writing to advise** in the light of these.

✔ Make a **spider diagram** of ideas and advice that you could give (see page 69).

✔ **Select** by **highlighting** the main points you want to use.

✔ **Plan** your points in a logical order.

# WRITING

## HOW TO WRITE YOUR RESPONSE

### Freedom's price tag

Exams will soon be over, and once they are you will be free; relaxing, having fun – partying, going shopping...BUT when the celebrations are over, the dawn of reality will come creeping over the horizon.

Fun and celebrations, CDs and clothes, all come with a price tag attached. So unless you've recently struck oil, funds will need to be generated and replenished. Let's face it, most ex-Year 11 students spend their long post-exam summer working to support their 'carefree' lifestyle...

> Catchy headline to create interest. This is a shopping metaphor – used later in the article, too.

> General introduction leading into the topic

> Informal friendly tone, using personal pronouns. Also suggests that everyone does this – readers would appreciate this

### One size doesn't fit all

When setting out to find a summer job, don't be lured into thinking that what suits your friends will necessarily suit you. 'Come and work with me at the stables – they need some extra help.' Sounds great? But wait a minute: do you really want to spend time mucking out smelly manure from under the sharp hooves of spirited steeds?

Think about what you want to do, but remember, it is only a temporary occupation, not a lifetime career. Try experimenting with something you might not otherwise do, which might give you a different type of experience. If you want to have a career in computer design, attached to a screen indoors all day, look for a job that means working with people, like a care assistant, or one that involves working outside, at your local garden centre for example. Interesting and unusual experiences like these will give you a different perspective on the world which, in the future, may prove invaluable...

> Sub-heading – refocuses reader and continues shopping metaphor

> 'Lured' – good use of vocabulary

> This question makes the reader think and agree

> Personal direction and use of present tense

> Useful, non threatening practical example that strengthens impact of the advice being given

> 'Carrot' approach tempting the reader (something in it for them)

### Why this is a good response

- It uses an appropriate informal tone.
- The writer uses a varied vocabulary and tone, e.g. **Let's face it** (informal) and **perspective** (formal and impressive).
- The shopping metaphor, adds interests, as does the alliteration in **spirited** and **steeds**.

- The advice given is expressed in a non-threatening way, using personal pronouns to address the reader directly.
- The present tense is used consistently.
- Headings and sub-headings indicate an understanding of how to draw in readers when writing an article.

 To test yourself, go to Writing – Writing to advise.

# WRITING TO ANALYSE, REVIEW, COMMENT

## Key features of this type of writing

**Intended reader:** someone who is **interested** in a topic or subject.

**Purpose:** to aid someone's **understanding**; to help clarify your own thoughts.

**Structure:** a **non-chronological** series of points that develop from one another in **logical** paragraphs.

**Language features** – these types of writing should:

- be impersonal (though sometimes personal)
- adopt a **formal** tone
- use the **present** tense
- contain **logical connectives** (link words) such as **alternatively, however, on the other hand**
- use **analytical markers** such as **in view of this, nevertheless, the evidence suggests, from another perspective**.

Each of these three types of writings is slightly different. An exam question may ask you to focus on just one of the three, or may ask you to combine two or all three (see below).

**Analyse:** you need to examine a topic in an impersonal way, considering a range of different opinions.

**Review:** you need to consider and assess the merits of something and/or the reasons for a point of view or a course of action.

**Comment:** you need to make observations on, and remarks about, a topic.

## HOW TO START

Look carefully at what the question is asking you to do.

> **Topic** that will be the focus of your writing

From sports to music to models – the media nowadays seems to create celebrities and superheroes for the public to admire. Choose one such 'superstar' who has caught your attention or imagination and consider the effect of the attention they receive.

> **Perspective** – from which you will be writing

> **Form** that your writing will take

Write an article for your local newspaper aimed at teenage readers in which you:

> **Intended readers**

- **analyse** why your chosen superstar is so popular
- **review** whether they deserve the attention and admiration they receive
- **comment** on the effect that the media's attention on the superstar creates on young people.

> **Purpose** – why you are writing

Spend about 45 minutes on this section.

## PLAN YOUR RESPONSE

There are **three** distinct stages in writing an article of this type – analysis, review and comment – and this needs to be reflected in your planning as well as in the article itself.

1 Choose a superstar on whom you would like to focus in your writing.

2 Make a **spider diagram analysing** the reasons why your chosen superstar has become a media celebrity.

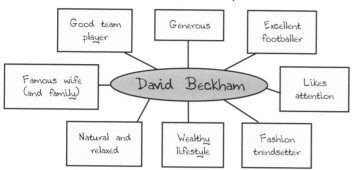

3 Pick out about three of these reasons and make a **bullet-pointed list reviewing** whether they demonstrate that the person deserves the admiration and status they receive:

> • Excellent footballer – yes, really is a great player
> • Fashion trendsetter – no, does it to attract attention to himself to get more money
> • Famous wife – they put themselves in the spotlight, but it has caused trouble.

4 Finally, **draw up a chart** picking out **comments** that could be made about the positive and negative effects that this celebrity status creates on young people.

| Positive effect | | | Negative effect |
|---|---|---|---|
| Inspires others to take up sport and play well | * | * | Makes it seem so easy to be brilliant |
| Interesting and creative | * | * | Young people follow fashion whether they can afford it or not |
| Role model to live up to – hard-working, married with kids | * | * | Makes young people dissatisfied – they don't have so much money |

## HOW TO START TO STRUCTURE YOUR RESPONSE

When you are writing your response to a task, remember:

- **the form** – this is a newspaper article
- **your readers** – teenagers
- **purpose** – to analyse the effect of celebrities on young people
- **the type of writing required** – analyse, review, and comment.

**Step one** – Introduce your celebrity and the topic.

*An eye-catching headline that plays on a well-known celebrity TV show*

> He's a celebrity
>
> should someone get him out of here?
>
> Hardly a day seems to go by without a picture of David Beckham in the newspaper, or a comment about him on the television or radio. He must be one of the most famous and popular celebrities in Britain, or even the world, today. The media has certainly played its part in putting him in the spotlight of everyone's attention. Nevertheless, one wonders why? Is it just because he is a talented footballer? Does he deserve this fame? And finally, what effect does the creation of such a superhero have on young people around the country?

*An introduction that outlines the topic to be discussed and highlights some of the issues through the use of questions*

**Step two** – Analyse why Beckham has become a media celebrity.

*Balanced analysis*

> Beckham's rise to celebrity status has come as a result of a combination of factors. No one doubts that his brilliant performance on the field singled him out for attention in the first place. Off the pitch he is a trendsetter; his distinctive haircuts are bound to get him noticed. His fashionable lifestyle and eye-catching, popstar wife attract the attention of the paparazzi wherever he goes and whatever he does. It is exactly the kind of thing everyone wants to read about, gloat over – envious or not...

*Formal, impersonal tone*

**Step three** – Review whether Beckham deserves his celebrity status.

*Maintains present tense*

> All this media attention has turned Beckham into a celebrity of superstar status in the eyes of the public. Teenagers in particular idolise him, but is he a deserving recipient of so much glory? Anyone who sees Beckham play is spellbound by his fancy footwork. He is also a good team player, who makes generous compliments about his fellow players. These are good qualities that deserve attention. On the other hand, there is no doubt that what he does off-the-pitch is designed to get him noticed, helping keep the money coming in from books and magazine fees...

*Alliteration to catch the reader's attention*

*Examination of Beckham's qualities*

# WRITING

**Step four** – **Comment on the effect created by the media on young people.**

> Is Beckham's fame good for teenagers?
>
> However, the attention created by the media has both advantages and disadvantages for Beckham's teenage fans. Certainly he has helped to revive teenagers' interest in the English football scene. He also inspires others to take up the sport he excels in. Followers of Beckham fashion have fun tying to keep up with the latest creations of their hero and the evidence suggests that he is a positive role model both on and off the pitch. On the other hand, he makes success seem so easy that those who try to follow in his footsteps and fail may be discouraged, feeling they are 'losers'...

*Use of sub-heading to refocus the reader's attention*

*Balanced comments giving different opinions*

**Step five** – **Bring your article to a rounded and effective conclusion.**

> Good or bad, the media, with all its attention on those who are deserving or undeserving, is here to stay. What is important is to put these superstars into a bigger picture of the world as a whole. Stars, like Beckham, somehow learn to live with seeing themselves on the pages of the latest glossy magazine. It is part of the price of fame and no one can really 'get them out of here'.

*Conclusion helps the reader to put the topic into perspective. It leaves them to draw their own conclusions. It ends with a reminder of the title.*

## Why this is a good response

- It address all three parts of the task.
- It appeals to the needs and interests of the teenage reader (the audience).
- It is clearly constructed, using link words such as **however** and **on the other hand**.

- It gives balanced opinions.
- It sustains an impersonal, formal tone and the use of the present tense.
- It uses devices such as rhetorical questions to add interest and involve the reader.

 To test yourself, go to Writing – Writing to analyse, review, comment .

# READING: MEDIA TEXTS

These sample questions are similar to those you may meet in your GCSE examination. Try answering the questions. When you have finished, compare your answers with those given on pages 100-121 to see how well you have done.

Answer all the questions in this section. Spend about **60 minutes** on it.

**Item I**

## Brother's plea to treat killer more humanely

**by Lyndsey Rawle**
lydndseyrawle@wakefieldexpress.co.uk

The brother of a multiple killer dubbed 'Hannibal the Cannibal' and caged in the dungeons of Wakefield prison has launched a campaign for more humane conditions.

Robert Mawdsley has spent most of his adult life in solitary confinement enclosed behind the walls of the high security building on Love Lane, nicknamed Monster Mansion.

The Channel Five programme Hideous Crimes highlighted the murderer's bizarre and tragic story and his family's plea to improve his quality of life.

Speaking to the Wakefield Express, Mawdsley's brother Paul, from Liverpool, said: "We accept he is not going to come out of prison but we think he should have the same regime as other prisoners."

Mawdsley, 49, was put in Broadmoor hospital in the late 1970s after garrotting a paedophile. What happened next is the stuff of prison legend but it's said that while at the high security hospital for the criminally insane he and another prisoner killed a man and Mawdsley ate his brain with a spoon.

He was transferred to Wakefield Prison shortly afterwards where he killed two inmates and gained his reputation as Britain's most dangerous prisoner.

A glass cage was made in the prison especially for Mawdsley in 1983.

"It's exactly like a cage," Paul added. "It was actually built for him – they decided there and then that was the best situation for him.

"We accept he can't mix with other prisoners.

"I don't suppose it matters exactly where he is. It's about the treatment he is getting and so that he is treated like a normal prisoner.

"He is kept in solitary confinement and he can't have any education or work.

"He needs a psychologist in there to find out what his problems are and what treatment he needs."

GLASS rage: Paul Mawdsley, campaigning for better treatment of his brother in Wakefield Prison. Pictures courtesy of Channel Five.

A spokeswoman from the prison service said she couldn't comment on individual cases.

Mr Mawdsley, speaking after last Tuesday's programme, added: "I'd like the prison service to stop and think about it."

He added: "You can't put a guy in solitary confinement for 25 years and just leave him."

## Item 2

# Death penalty call renewed

The death penalty should be "available" to the UK justice system for use in the most heinous of crimes, according to Ann Widdecombe.

" If you can save life by having a death penalty... there is an argument to be made "
Ann Widdecombe

The Tory former Home Office minister made the claim as heightened emotion over the murders of Cambridgeshire's Jessica Chapman and Holly Wells has prompted commentators across the nation to consider the return of capital punishment for child killers.

Ben Page, from pollsters MORI, said that three-quarters of the population consistently say they believe the death penalty is "suitable in some circumstances".

But the Bishop of Durham, the Rt Rev Michail Turnbull, said a return to state execution would mean society admitting defeat.

### Save innocent lives

Miss Widdecombe, a Catholic and a supporter of a ban on hunting, said she had never believed in using the death penalty as a means of retribution.

She told BBC Radio 4's *Today* programme: "Now if you can save life by having a death penalty, regardless of what the methods used are... then I would maintain that there is an argument to be made."

### Remove rituals

Limits to the type of punishment would need to be made to ensure that it was not "long and protracted and exceptionally cruel".

"I would also like some of the ritual to go away," said the Maidstone and the Weald MP.

Miss Widdecombe said she did not believe juries would be unwilling to find a defendant guilty if they knew he would be executed.

### High emotion

The Rt Rev Turnbull said a time of high emotion, generated by public anger to the deaths of Holly and Jessica, was not the time to make radical changes to the law.

He said using capital punishment would rule out the chance of rehabilitating offenders – an essential element of current sentencing.

"If we are admitting defeat by putting the death penalty into place and killing off those who have committed dreadful crimes, then I think that is detriment of society as it stands," he told *Today*.

In 1969, Parliament voted to suspend the death penalty indefinitely. Repeated calls for its return have been consistently rejected but a mandatory life sentence was introduced in its place.

## Questions

Read Item 1, a newspaper article from *The Wakefield Express*.

1. **These questions are concerned with fact and opinion.**

   a. How does Paul Mawdsley use facts and opinions to argue for better conditions for his brother?

   b. Explain the way language is used by the reporter to create an impression of Robert Mawdsley.

Read Item 2, a BBC web page. It is a news item written shortly after the murders of schoolgirls Jessica Chapman and Holly Wells.

2. **This question is concerned with following an argument and selecting appropriate material.**

   Does the report support or oppose the death penalty? How are the arguments presented?

3. **This question is asking you to compare these two texts.**

   a. Compare the texts, by examining their:
   • purpose and audience
   • layout and presentation.

   b. Which text is more successful, and why?

# POETRY FROM DIFFERENT CULTURES AND TRADITIONS

**Question 1: What can we learn about lives in different countries and cultures from 'Blessing' by Imtiaz Dharker and one other poem you have studied?**

### Blessing

The skin cracks like a pod.
There never is enough water.

Imagine the drip of it,
The small splash, echo
in a tin mug,
the voice of a kindly god.

Sometimes, the sudden rush
of fortune. The municipal pipe bursts,
silver crashes to the ground
and the flow has found
a roar of tongues. From the huts,
a congregation: every man woman
child for streets around
butts in, with pots,
brass, copper, aluminium,
plastic buckets,
frantic hands,

and naked children
screaming in the liquid sun,
Their highlights polished to perfection,
flashing light,
as the blessing sings
over their small bones.

*Imtiaz Dharker*

*This is a possible poem to choose for comparison – the exemplar answers are based around this.*

### Two scavengers in a truck,
 ### Two beautiful people in a Mercedes

At the stoplight waiting for the light
            nine a.m. downtown San Francisco
   a bright yellow garbage truck
        with two garbagemen in red plastic blazers
      standing on the back stoop
            one on each side holding on
   and looking down into
               an elegant open Mercedes
with an elegant couple in it

The man
   in a hip three-piece linen suit
        with shoulder-length blond hair and sunglasses
The young blond woman so casually coifed
            with a short skirt and colored stockings
   on the way to his architect's office

And the two scavengers up since four a.m.
               grungy from their route
         on the way home
The older of the two with iron grey hair
               and hunched back
      looking down like some
               gargoyle Quasimodo
And the younger of the two
            also with sunglasses & long hair
      about the same age as the Mercedes driver

And both scavengers gazing down
               as from a great distance
      at the cool couple
   as if they were watching some odourless TV ad
         in which everything is always possible

And the very red light for an instant
         holding all four close together
      as if anything at all were possible
               between them
   across that small gulf
         in the high seas
               of this democracy

*Lawrence Ferlinghetti*

**Question 2: Examine the way in which the poets present the experience of being caught between two cultures in 'Presents from my aunts in Pakistan' and one other poem you have studied.**

### Presents from my aunts in Pakistan

They sent me a salwar kameez
    peacock-blue,
      and another
   glistening like an orange split open,
embossed slippers, gold and black
     points curling.
  Candy-striped glass bangles
     snapped, drew blood.
Like at school, fashions changed
    in Pakistan –
the salwar bottoms were broad and stiff,
    then narrow.
My aunts chose an apple-green sari,
   silver-bordered
     for my teens.

I tried each satin-silken top –
  was alien in the sitting-room.
I could never be as lovely
    as those clothes –
  I longed
for denim and corduroy.
  My costume clung to me
    and I was aflame,
I couldn't rise up out of its fire,
  half-English,
    unlike Aunt Jamila.

I wanted my parents' camel-skin lamp –
  switching it on in my bedroom,
to consider the cruelty
    and the transformation
from camel to shade,
  marvel at the colours
    like stained glass.

My mother cherished her jewellery –
  Indian gold, dangling, filigree.
    But it was stolen from our car.
The presents were radiant in my wardrobe.
  My aunts requested cardigans
   from Marks and Spencers.

My salwar kameez
  didn't impress the schoolfriend
Who sat on my bed, asked to see
  my weekend clothes.
But often I admired the mirror-work,
  tried to glimpse myself
    in the miniature
glass circles, recall the story
  how the three of us
    sailed to England.
Prickly heat had me screaming on the way.
  I ended up in a cot
in my English grandmother's dining-room,
  found myself alone,
    playing with a tin boat.

I pictured my birthplace
  from fifties photographs.
    When I was older
there was a conflict, a fractured land
  throbbing through newsprint.
Sometimes I saw Lahore –
    my aunts in shaded rooms,
screened from male visitors,
  sorting presents,
    wrapping them in tissue.

Or there were beggars, sweeper girls
  and I was there –
    of no fixed nationality,
staring through fretwork
    at the Shalimar Gardens.

*Moniza Alvi*

*This is a possible poem to choose for comparison – the exemplar answers are based around this.*

**Half-caste**

Excuse me
standing on one leg
I'm half-caste
Explain yuself
wha yu mean
when yu say half-caste
yu mean when Picasso
mix red an green
is a half-caste canvas/
Explain yuself
wha yu mean
when yu say half-caste
yu mean when light an shadow
mix in de sky
is a half-caste weather/
Well in dat case
england weather
nearly always half-caste
in fact some o dem cloud
half-caste till dem overcast
so spiteful dem don't want de sun pass
ah rass/
Explain yuself
wha yu mean
when yu say half-caste
yu mean tchaikovsky
sit dowm at dah piano
an mix a black key
wid a white key
is a half-caste symphony/

Explain yuself
wha yu mean
Ah listening to yu wid de keen
half of mih ear
Ah looking at yu wid de keen
half of mih eye
and when I'm introduced to yu
I'm sure you'll
understand
why I offer yu half-a-hand
an when I sleep at night
I close half-a-eye
consequently when I dream
I dream half-a-dream
an when moon begin to glow
I half-caste human being
cast half-a-shadow
but yu must come back tomorrow
wid de whole of yu eye
an de whole of yu ear
an de whole of yu mind
an I will tell yu
de other half
of my story

*John Agard*

## WRITING

**Answer one question from the following:**

1. The government is considering changing the law, so that parents will no longer be allowed to hit their children.

   Write a letter to the Prime Minister, where you **argue** the case that no one should be allowed to smack children.

2. A recent report has shown that teenagers are less healthy than ever before.

   Write an article for a school magazine, to **persuade** students to eat more healthily.

3. People enjoy going to different places for interest and amusement. **Describe** a place that has made you feel happy.

4. Choose a sport, hobby or a way of passing the time that you enjoy. **Explain** why you enjoy it.

- Compare your answer to each question with the sample student answers provided. The answers provided would have been awarded D to B grades. In each case the answer has been annotated to show you how an examiner would begin to assess each answer.

- Try to decide whether your own answer is at the same grade as the one given by adding similar annotations to your own answer. Then read through 'What is good about this answer' and check whether your answer includes many of these same aspects.

- Now look at 'How this answer could be improved'. If your own answer contains many of the points listed here, then it would be awarded a higher grade than the sample student answer.

- Finally, read and think about all the bullet points listed under 'Don't forget...'.

## READING: MEDIA TEXTS

> **Question 1a: How does Paul Mawdsley use facts and opinions to argue for better conditions for his brother?**

### D grade response

*General statement to begin*

Paul Mawdsley uses a mixture of facts and opinions to make his argument seem convincing.

*Identifies opinions*

*Comments*

*Main point in the argument*

He gives an opinion when he says: ' ...we think he should have the same regime as other prisoners'. This is to make his brother seem just like any other prisoner. Also, he says that Robert is kept in something 'exactly like a cage', which is another opinion.

*Some involvement in the argument*

*Further involvement*

In his opinion, the prison guards thought this was right for Robert and even he thinks Robert can't mix with other prisoners. He just wants his brother to be normal. Another opinion is that Robert should have a psychologist to find out the treatment he needs. This seems quite convincing, because he ought to be looked after.

*Organised: moving from opinions to facts*

Paul finishes with an opinion that makes people think: ' You can't put a guy in solitary confinement for 25 years and just leave him.'

There aren't as many facts as opinions. This is because Paul is trying to persuade us his argument is right.

*Opinion not fact?*

*Facts identified*

*Comment*

He does use a few facts though. He says that the prison guards thought straight away the glass cage was the best situation for him. Also, he says that Robert is kept in solitary confinement and he can't have any education or work. These are terrible facts. No one would want to spend all their life in a glass case on their own with nothing to do.

*Conclusion fails to deal with the question*

That's how they keep Robert Mawdsley because he has killed people and has eaten their brains.

# EXAM PRACTICE: ANSWERS

## What is good about this answer

- The student makes clear the link between the facts and opinions and the idea that Paul Mawdsley is arguing for better conditions.
- Opinions and facts are identified. In only one case – 'the prison guards thought straight away the glass cage was the best situation for him' – might there be any disagreement. It is unlikely this point could be proved; and we can assume that some thought did go into the solution. Paul's statement, therefore, is an opinion.
- There are several comments on facts and opinions that help to indicate how Paul Mawdsley is arguing. There are attempts to explain their effect on the audience.
- Rather than simply working through what Paul Mawdsley has to say, the student clearly divides the response into two sections: facts and opinions.
- With the exception of the final sentence, the response is appropriate, dealing with what Paul Mawdsley says, rather than the reporter's view of events or just the story.

## How this answer could be improved

- Each fact and opinion tends to be dealt with in isolation. If the student had shown understanding of how they work together, the grade would have been higher. He might have pointed out, for example, that Paul Mawdsley tries to make us feel sorry for his brother, by concentrating on his treatment rather than his crimes, so that his argument is not undermined.
- The over-arching point could also be made that the selective facts and opinions are supported by an appearance that Paul Mawdsley is very reasonable (in his opinion, Robert cannot mix with other prisoners).
- Some facts and opinions are presented without comment. Explaining their effect would further impress the examiner.
- The student presents one opinion as a fact, and loses focus on the question in the final sentence. A conclusion that summed up how Paul Mawdsley uses facts and opinions would have been more effective.

## Don't forget...when examining the use of facts and opinions

- Answer the question that has been set. No credit is given for irrelevant material.
- Stay focused on the task and ensure your comments are appropriate.
- Identify facts and opinions correctly.
- Make a point clearly before introducing the evidence such as a quotation.
- Show understanding of how facts and opinions are used, rather than simply pointing them out.
- Produce an overview of how facts and opinions have been used (relate them to the purpose of the text); then base what you say later upon that initial analysis (e.g. 'Paul Mawdsley tries to gain sympathy for his brother... This is how the facts and opinions he has used help to support that aim...').

**Question 1b: Explain the way language is used by the reporter to create an impression of Robert Mawdsley.**

### C grade response

*Clear comment on language to begin*

*Further comment*

Robert Mawdsley seems like a wild animal because he is 'caged'. Also, you think that he leads a very miserable life because of the word that makes it sound like he is in an old castle and is being tortured – 'dungeons'.

*Working through relevant section of article*

He is also kept in a place called 'Monster Mansion', so that does not seem very nice. The prison is a bit like something in the 'Adams Family' and Mawdsley is made out to be a monster.

*Further impression of Mawdsley*

*Identifies language*

*Comments on 'plea'*

The reporter says Robert Mawdsley has had a bizarre and tragic story and his family is making a 'plea' to have his quality of life improved – like his brother is making a 'plea' in the headline – and we imagine they are really begging, so this must mean a lot to them.

*Use of appropriate vocabulary to identify an effect*

There is also language that deals with what Mawdsley did to get himself in a glass case. There are phrases like 'garrotting a paedophile' and 'killed a man and ate his brain with a spoon'. This language is emotive because it touches our emotions when we read it and that affects what we think about Mawdsley.

*Appropriate quotation and comment to conclude*

The reporter also calls him 'Britain's most dangerous prisoner'. This opinion encourages us to continue reading the article because he seems very important and frightening.

# EXAM PRACTICE: ANSWERS

**What is good about this answer**

- All the material selected is **appropriate and is used effectively** in responding to the question.
- The student focuses on what **impression** of Mawdsley is being created.
- Quotations are clearly identified in almost all cases, and comments are clear. The points about Mawdsley **are never confusing**.
- Comments often deal with **what the language implies**, rather than just summarising what is said. Because the student is showing a greater understanding, it will increase the mark awarded.
- Since she has to handle relatively little text, the student sensibly **works through it in order** and omits few relevant quotations.
- Whether it was intentional or not, the answer has a **final paragraph that serves as a conclusion** – and the final three words sum up the impression of the prisoner that has been created in the first half of the article.

**How this answer could be improved**

- Although the language can be dealt with as it occurs in the article, **an opening statement** about what overall impression is being created would have given greater structure to the answer. Later points could then be seen to be adding to that profile of Mawdsley.
- **Extra points** could have been included – for example, the fact that he is first described as a 'multiple killer', and that there is irony since the prison is on 'Love Lane'.
- At times, the student's own **expression is limited**. It is also rather too informal (e.g. 'nice', 'a bit', 'made out') where an analytical style would be more appropriate. More formal expression throughout would have created a better impression on the examiner.
- The point about how the emotive language affects us **needs further explanation**.
- Some **important language** is not explained, such as 'ate his brains with a spoon'. The phrase 'ate his brains...' makes the incident seem more horrible by being described in such everyday language.

**Don't forget...when analysing the use of language**

- Identify **relevant quotations** and comment clearly on their meaning and/or effect.
- **Relate what you say** to the question.
- **Use technical vocabulary** when appropriate – as the student does here with 'emotive'. She might have also used 'metaphor' and 'alliteration' when discussing 'Monster Mansion'. In exam articles you might also find examples of similes or onomatopoeia to discuss.
- Examine the language in depth, and avoid vague and relatively meaningless generalisations such as 'The language is varied and affects the reader by making him think about the person being described'. **By being more precise** you will gain higher marks.

**Question 2: Does the report support or oppose the death penalty? How are the arguments presented?**

*Responds directly to question*

*Indicates the structure of the text*

*Focus on method used to give credibility to Widdecombe's views*

*Understanding of how language used and argumentative technique*

*Recognition that there is no proof*

*Facts to support her point of view*

*Other side of argument*

*Linguistic technique recognised and explained*

*Points he uses to develop his viewpoint*

## B grade response

The report presents both sides of the argument. Although it begins by explaining Ann Widdecombe's views that the death penalty should be reintroduced, it ends with the views of the Bishop of Durham, who thinks we should not change the current situation.

Ann Widdecombe is presented as a balanced person who opposes fox hunting and is religious, so when she speaks in favour of the death penalty, we are more likely to believe her.

She says it should be available for the worst crimes. Calling them 'heinous' makes them sound very serious and evil. She also anticipates possible disagreements with what she is saying by pointing out that a move back to capital punishment would not stop juries from convicting criminals. However, her opinion is just that - an opinion.

However, she is supported by MORI. They add the fact that three-quarters of the population believe the death penalty is 'suitable in some circumstances'.

Only the Bishop of Durham, Michael Turnbull, speaks against her. At the start, he says the reintroduction would be a 'defeat' for society, making it seem a battle has been lost. Later, he makes several apparently sensible points, saying it is a bad time because people are outraged about the murder of the two girls. Also, as a religious figure, he says that we should try to rehabilitate offenders, not kill them. He thinks that society would be damaged if it did not try to help the criminals, even those who have committed 'dreadful crimes'.

## What is good about this answer

- The answer begins with a **sensible introduction**, responding directly to the title and identifying the two sides in the report.
- The relevant points have been **identified and organised**, so that one side of the argument is handled and then the other.
- As well as locating the important ideas, the student has explained some of them so that he **deals with the method** of the writer – for instance, how Ann Widdecombe is described and why; the importance of particular words (e.g. 'heinous' and 'defeat'); and the effect of some facts and opinions.
- The opening paragraph gives an **impression of structure** in what has been produced: the fact that one point of view is prominent at the beginning but that the other features at the end.

## How this answer could be improved

- The idea in the opening paragraph could have been developed to explain the effect of opening with one viewpoint but finishing with another. **A judgement** could have been made about where this places the emphasis.
- Similarly, there could have been a **commentary** on how *effectively* each point is made, to accompany the explanations of what is being suggested.
- Some points **lack development**. For example, the mention of the effect on juries would benefit from further explanation. In this case, it is a disputed point, not made clear in the report itself, that juries might be reluctant to sentence individuals to death because it is so final; whereas they might be happier to sentence someone to imprisonment.
- **Sensible reactions** by the student are not always made clear to the reader. When, for instance, we read 'her opinion is just that – an opinion', we must reflect upon it to understand what the student is trying to say (presumably, that an argument is more convincing if facts support opinions).
- At the end, Michael Turnbull's arguments are listed rather than analysed. **Saying why each one has been included** would have made this a better answer.
- A conclusion, perhaps giving a **personal view** of which side of the argument has been most convincing, would have been an improvement.

## Don't forget…when analysing how arguments are presented

- Read the text carefully and ensure you understand the points being made. If necessary, **highlight or list them** to create a plan.
- **Organise the material logically** so you are not going back and forth between points of view.
- **Examine how the argument has been constructed** – do not simply repeat what it says.
- **Consider the impact of language**, structure, facts and opinions, examples, anecdotes, quotations, and so on. Explain why they have been used and what they suggest to the reader.
- Try to **set out your main idea(s)** in an introduction and sum up what you have discovered in a conclusion.

# EXAM PRACTICE: ANSWERS

Question 3a: Compare the texts, by examining their:
• purpose and audience
• layout and presentation

## D grade response

*Identifies purpose*

*Identifies audience*

*Involves appeal*

'Brother's plea to treat killer more humanely' is an article from a newspaper. It is designed to be read by anyone who buys the paper regularly or picks it up to read. It is trying to attract people who like horror stories because it talks about 'Hannibal the Cannibal' (that might also attract those who have seen the film) and he is also described as a 'killer' in the title.

*Second purpose and audience*

*Some personal response*

*Further identification of audience*

The BBC web page is obviously written for people who have the Internet and who are interested in news. I think that might be adults because it is not really very interesting. I don't know who Ann W is, and the Bishop sounds really boring. Only people who are really interested in finding out what people think about things are likely to read a report like this one.

*Presentation*

*Effects, linked to detail*

*Touch of comment*

Because the 'Brother's plea' article is in black and white, it isn't very attractive. The picture of Robert's brother makes him seem as if he is just an ordinary man because he has a denim jacket and his head shaved. It looks as though he has a nice house. The big headline attracts us at first and the bit about 'GLASS rage' stands out at the bottom, though it doesn't make much sense.

*A comparison made, with comment*
*Comments on details*
*Ranges across devices used*
*Again, simple comment*
*Aware of other elements*

The web page is more fun because it's in colour, but Ann Widdecombe looks plastic. The headline is small and is not very dramatic, but there is a big coloured speech by Ann W which stands out and makes you read it.

# EXAM PRACTICE: ANSWERS

## What is good about this answer

- The **purpose and audience** are identified in both texts.
- When dealing with purpose and audience, **reasons are given** why these texts would be appropriate by mentioning some language in 'Brother's plea' and the importance of Ann Widdecombe in defining who is likely to read the web page.
- **Presentational devices** are also identified, and there is some comment on their effect.
- The **comments are relatively simple** ('it is not really very interesting') but also show the student's personal involvement ('I think that').
- **There is some comparison** – mainly by juxtaposition (setting one idea against another, in this case contrasting paragraphs).
- Both the bullet points **are dealt with** on both texts.

## How this answer could be improved

- The student has missed the opportunity to link the various strands of the question, which could have been achieved by writing about how the layout and presentation are used for a specific purpose to **attract the potential audience**.
- As this is a question involving comparison, there should have been **more linking of features** in the two texts. Where ideas are not linked a D grade is normally awarded; using a comparative vocabulary, such as: 'In comparison...', 'On the other hand...', 'Similarly...', 'Although the first text...', 'the second text...', 'In a similar way, the second text...'; and comparative words like 'bigger', 'clearer', 'more obvious' gain greater credit.
- The actual audiences could have been made more precise by a more careful examination of the **kinds of vocabulary** used.
- **Layout** was largely ignored.
- Some **presentational devices** were mentioned but others, such as the caption, were not.
- When writing about media, higher grades will be awarded for **using media terminology**. For example, the use of 'pull-quote' rather than 'a big coloured speech'.
- Abbreviations like 'Ann W' make it seem that the student is **writing notes** and it won't impress the examiner.

## Don't forget…when comparing texts and writing about purpose and audience, layout and presentation

- Make sure your comparisons are clear: use **the correct vocabulary**.
- Use technical vocabulary whenever it is appropriate.
- Justify your decisions about purpose and audience by **reference to the texts**, rather than by generalising.
- Avoid simply describing what is there. Concentrate instead on **analysing the features**, particularly when writing about layout and presentation.
- Do not be afraid to **make judgements on the texts** (i.e. include your own opinions), but support these with evidence from the texts.
- Ensure you deal with **the stem of the question** and each bullet point.
- Try to cover each element in the question **in equal detail**.

# EXAM PRACTICE: ANSWERS

### Question 3b: Which text is more successful, and why?

**C grade response**

*Begins with a general introduction*

Both the texts are successful because they appeal to their audiences. The newspaper article is perfect for a newspaper and the web page is what you would expect to find on the Internet.

*Responds directly to question: opinion offered*

*Justifies opinion*

*Involves presentation as well as language*

*Definite judgement*

However, I think the newspaper article is the most successful. Firstly, if you found it you would want to read it because the man in the pictures looks a bit sad, and you want to find out what has happened. Secondly, it talks about horrible prisons and about eating brains with a spoon, and people reading the newspaper would want to know about that sort of thing. The headline is not perfect because some people won't know what 'humanely' means, so they could be put off, but I think most newspaper readers would give this article a try.

*Comparison made*

*Opinion explained*

*Positive view*

*Critical view*

*Links back to target audience*

I'm not so sure about the web page – it seems boring. Although it is for people who are older, I can't imagine why anyone would want to read it because it doesn't have a story and talks about the death penalty without any pictures of it or stories about people being hung or gassed. The colour would make some people decide to read it, and if you knew who Ann Widdecombe was you might be interested. I think it is just right for older people, but not for me.

*Another comparison and links texts*

*A final evaluation*

Overall, both the texts are successful in what they try to do, which is to make us think about murderers and how they should be treated. It is simply that they are aimed at different audiences, so it depends how they react. It seems a pity there isn't a picture of the murderer in the newspaper or some more interesting stories in the web page. Then they would both be better.

## What is good about this answer

- The student deals with success and **how the success is achieved**.
- Although the introduction indicates that both texts have qualities, there is then a section in which the student begins to evaluate the chosen article and say why it is best, in **direct response to the question**.
- The opinion is supported by **reference to the text** and deals with both language and presentation.
- **Comparison is clearly attempted:** 'I'm not so sure about the web page...'
- **The opinion is explained** – why the text might be successful and why it might not be are both included.
- Both the second and third paragraphs link what has been said back to **the requirements of the question**.
- The conclusion links the two texts again (they 'make us think about murderers and how they should be treated'), balances the two texts and moves to a final judgement, which comments clearly – and briefly – on **how the texts could have been improved**.

## How this answer could be improved

- There are many areas of the texts that could also have been commented upon, such as other **presentational devices or a wider range of language**.
- At times the personal aspect of the review is given too much importance ('...so they could be put off, but I think...'), and **a more analytical approach** would have been better in places, for example: 'There are several features which might not appeal to the reader of a tabloid newspaper, such as...').
- The language used tends to be too casual and informal ('I'm not so sure...'). More **formal language usually leads to a more precise analysis**.
- **The response seems to contradict itself** by firstly saying both texts are successful and then making critical comments about the web page being 'boring'.
- Overall, the answer says too much about what is missing and what might have improved the texts, rather than the many more **positive features** that could have been discussed.

## Don't forget...when writing about the success of a text or texts

- Success will almost always be related to **purpose and audience**. Do not try to respond without discussing these important features.
- Be precise. Use **details from the texts** rather than simply giving unsupported views. **Remember: 'Point, evidence, comment'**.
- Use **appropriate language and/or technical terms** when you can, and standard English throughout.
- If you are dealing with two texts, **compare them clearly** with balanced comments.
- In general, try to use details from the texts that you have not already written about in other answers. Feel free to **range across all the features** of the given texts, including how arguments have been put together, the uses of facts and opinions, and so on.
- **Analysis and evaluation** (*how* the texts 'work' and whether they work well) will always be marked higher than descriptive answers which simply say what the texts contain.

## POETRY

> **Question 1: What can we learn about lives in different countries and cultures from 'Blessing' by Imtiaz Dharker and one other poem you have studied?**

### D grade response

*Links with title*

The poems, 'Blesssing' and 'Two Scavengers', are set in different countries in different parts of the world. In both poems there are people who don't seem to have much money.

*Awareness of culture*

'Two Scavengers' is set in San Francisco, USA, and it describes garbage men and rich people beside them in a car. We can see there is a difference between the rich people and the poor in the USA.

*Quotation for evidence*

*Some development of ideas*

The garbage men are 'scavengers'. They collect the rubbish and so they are dirty: 'grungy from their route.' They do not seem to have a good life. They have to get up early (4am) and have uncomfortable clothes which are very bright, 'red plastic blazers'. They cannot even sit down in their truck – they just have to hold on to the back part as it moves down the street.

*Double meaning?*

*Interpreting the poem*

*Appropriate details from the poem*

The dustmen look down on the rich people in the Mercedes. The man and woman both have smart clothes and look elegant. They must spend money on how they look because she is 'casually coifed' and has a short skirt and stockings. The man 'has a three-piece linen suit'. It says he's on the way to work in an 'architect's office'.

*Still responding to title*

*Comments on the language used and gives some interpretation*

The poem tells us about how the people look. One of the 'scavengers' has 'iron grey hair' and this makes him sound very old. He might have had a hard life because he looks like a 'Quasimodo', which sounds like a frightening character from a film. The younger garbage man has 'sunglasses + long hair' like the rich man in the car, but his hair might be messy and he could look very scruffy.

# EXAM PRACTICE: ANSWERS

*Attempts to interpret how the poet has used language*

The poet uses alliteration to describe the people in the car – they are a 'cool couple'. They have more money than the ones on the truck and so they ignore them. The poet repeats the word 'elegant' to describe them, which makes it stand out.

*Compares the poems*

*Aware of religion/culture*

The people in 'Blessing' are different, and the poem has lots of emotion as it describes people celebrating when they have the water they need. It is set in a country like India or Pakistan where it is very hot and there isn't much fresh clean water. So having water becomes like a religious experience to them, which is why the poet calls them a 'congregation' and the water a 'blessing'.

*Extending ideas*

*Understands emotions*

The people suffer through lack of water and they sometimes dream about it: 'Imagine the drip of it...'They are poor, as well, because they only have tin mugs. They get water from a 'municipal pipe'. When it bursts, they catch the water in anything they can find and seem frantic for it. That is because it is so horribly hot. The water is really important for them. It's like a treasure. It is 'silver', as far as they are concerned.

*Supports the point*

*Aware of features of language*

*Attempts to explain effect*

The language of the poem makes everything rushed when the pipe bursts. There is a metaphor 'liquid sun' and a simile 'like a pod'. This language brings the scene to life so we know the sun is hot and their skin is dry.

*Summary to conclude*

In conclusion, the people in the two poems are quite different but we can find out lots of things about their lives and their cultures in the poems.

# EXAM PRACTICE: ANSWERS

Some good points about this response
- The student **responds directly to the question**. Rather than just writing all he knows about the poems, he writes about people, cultures, beliefs and the language used.
- The quotations and references are appropriate, and **evidence is given** to support the points made.
- The response shows an **awareness of ideas and feelings** in the poems, rather than just explaining what the poem says.
- The student is able to comment on the language – with some explanation, for example, of 'Quasimodo' – and is aware of **the effects created** at different times such as describing the people in 'Blessing' as 'frantic'.
- There is some **simple comparison**, showing the student is able to link ideas and situations: 'In both poems there are people who don't seem to have much money; 'The people in "Blessing" are different.'
- **Quotations are sometimes integrated** into the body of the response: 'which is why the poet calls them a "congregation" and the water a "blessing"'.

How this response could be improved
- Some ideas need to be more **closely examined** to show real understanding: for example, explaining the double meaning behind the words 'looking down' – the garbage men are 'looking down' on the couple, but in social terms their situations would be reversed. There could also have been a comment about how, for example, the clothes set the different people apart.
- Discussing the **effect of listing** of vessels used when the pipe bursts: how the best came first and the cheapest last, and what that implies would have been useful.
- Comments on the way language is used needs more development. Simply identifying similes and metaphors is not enough. The student needs to **explain why figurative language has been used**, and its effect.
- Points could have been made about **the poems' layouts** – for instance, how the lines are set out in 'Two Scavengers' to demonstrate the variations in the society and how it is not all neatly ordered and equally structured.
- Much closer comparison – of **details, features of the cultures and peoples' lives and the language** – would have improved the grade awarded.

Don't forget...what you need to do when writing about poetry from different cultures
- **Respond to the title**, rather than just 'translating' the poems into your own words.
- Remember to include mention of *what* the poems say but also *how* they say it.
- Make sure that your points are supported by **evidence from the poem**, usually a quotation, and add a **comment** about it.
- **Keep quotations brief** and don't use them more than once.
- **Make comparisons** between the poems whenever you can as this is recognised as a higher order skill.
- Try to **respond equally** to both poems.
- Prepare for the exam by completing **timed practice questions** so that you get used to including all your points in the time available.

**Question 2: Examine the way in which the poets present the experience of being caught between two cultures in 'Presents from my aunts in Pakistan' and one other poem you have studied.**

### B grade response

*Focus on the question*

'Presents from my aunts in Pakistan' and 'Half-caste' are both concerned with people who are caught between two cultures. However, where John Agard's poem seems angry because of the way mixed-race people are treated by society, Moniza Alvi depicts confusion - trapped between two cultures and unable to fit properly into either of them.

*Poems cross-referenced*

*Explains situations and introduces main points to be considered*

*Alvi's poem*

The narrator in Moniza Alvi's first-person poem is caught in a family situation where she feels excluded from both her British and Pakistani heritage. She understands the richness of the society of Pakistan where she was born, which is represented by the salwar kameez, the embossed slippers, and the vivid colours. It all sounds beautiful, yet: 'the candy-striped glass bangles/snapped, drew blood' and that hurt her.

*Appropriate details from poem*

*Suggests understanding of writer's techniques*

She feels isolated, unable to impress her school friend with the satin-silken clothes and saris, that her aunts have sent from Pakistan. She longs instead 'for denim and corduroy'. The past world of her parents, which she left as a baby, is remembered only through photographs. So she feels excluded from this old culture, as well as the new one in England: 'I couldn't rise up out of its fire/half-English'.

*Develops ideas and integrates quotations*

*Appreciates poet's situation*

The poem ends symbolically with her feelings of exclusion as she sees herself: 'of no fixed nationality,/staring through fretwork/at the Shalimar Gardens.'

*Compares Agard*

The voice in John Agard's poem 'Half-caste' also feels excluded, but he is not so accepting. He challenges the people who insult him by calling him half-caste: 'explain yuself/wha yu mean'.

*Effective use of textual detail*

Unlike the narrator in Alvi's poem, this person is not confused about his identity; he declares it is others who have got it wrong. He tries to explain that the whole world is made up of mixtures of colours, but we do not call them half-caste, and so he is asking why we put that name on people: 'well in dat case/england weather/nearly always half-caste'.

*Contrasting situation*

*Point clearly made*

We don't talk about half-caste weather, so we should not talk about half-caste people.

*Evidence*

# EXAM PRACTICE: ANSWERS

*Clear comparison*

*Comments on the main idea*

Alvi's narrator simply wants to be accepted for the person her dual cultural parentage has created, but Agard's is sarcastic and angry about the fact that he is not accepted as an equal: 'I half-caste human being/cast half-a-shadow'.

He is laughing at those who put him down by making his situation seem ridiculous.

*Further comparison*

*Language points*

*Interprets the feelings expressed in the poem*

*Attempts to explain layout*

The other big difference between the poems is their language and form. Agard writes in a conversational tone, using dialect, 'dem' instead of 'them' and 'ah rass' instead of 'our race'. The poem looks very solid and together. In fact, he does not even use full stops, perhaps to show that he is different from what is thought of as normal. We have to understand what he is saying by the way he has used the lines and the alternative breaks '/'.

*Explanation*

*Appropriate detail and explanation*

We are not supposed to think that he is uneducated, though, because he talks about Picasso and Tchaikovsky, and his ideas are clever: laughing at us by saying he is only half a person with half an eye and half a hand, and so on. He keeps repeating 'half' to remind us of how silly it is to label someone 'half-caste'.

*Comparison*

*Understands technique*

*Brief comment on verse*

In contrast, 'Presents from my aunts' presents a disjointed picture on the page, with lines almost randomly starting at different points and that shows her life is uneven. It uses colourful images such as the simile 'like an orange split open' and the metaphor 'I was aflame' to show the culture's life and how it burns her, she cannot be like a phoenix.

*Sums up and compares situations to conclude*

There is suffering in both poems - the narrator in Agard's poem hates being 'half-caste' and the confusion in Alvi's poem arising from the expectations of the two cultures to which she belongs. At the end, Alvi is stuck where she began, 'of no fixed nationality'. Agard says that tomorrow he will tell: 'de other half/of my story', suggesting we ought to realise he is more than half a man. He hopes we will have learned from what he says, but nothing will improve for Alvi.

## Some good points about this response

- The first paragraph deals with the title, links the poems and provides an **introduction for the response.**
- The student appreciates **how the poets present the cultures**. For example, the second paragraph notes how the presents represent Pakistani culture, and how the bangles, whilst pretty, actually cause problems for the girl by implying they represent her former culture.
- Quotations are often integrated into the response, rather than seeming like just a selected and individual example to prove a point. The student appears in **charge of the ideas**, has taken all of them in and processed the material.
- There is **effective cross-referencing** so that a point on one poem links with the other poem: 'In contrast, "Presents from my aunts"...', 'The other big difference between the poems is...', and so on.
- There is the **beginning of an analysis**: 'So she feels excluded from this old culture, as well as the new one in England'.
- The student gives the impression she knows **what the writer was setting out to achieve**, and the methods used.

## How this response could be improved

- Some points could be **explored in more depth**: for example, the point about the bangles could be related to the school friend's opinions of the clothes, and to how the poet cannot get a clear image of herself in the mirror-work.
- **Analysis of both writers' techniques** could be developed. For example, the 'symbolic' ending of 'Presents from my aunts' could be explained more clearly (the writer is outside both societies and can only look on, as if behind barriers).
- The response could be extended by simply saying more about **the poetic techniques** in both poems, in particular how repetition is used by Agard; how both poets use poetic devices; and how the reader reacts to different features of the poems.

## Don't forget...what you need to do when writing about poetry from different cultures

- **Respond to the title**, rather than just 'translating' the poems into your own words.
- Remember to include mention of **what the poems say but also how** they say it.
- Make sure that your points are supported by **evidence from the poem**, usually a quotation, and add a comment about it.
- **Keep quotations brief** and don't use them more than once.
- **Make comparisons** between the poems whenever you can as this is recognised as a higher-order skill.
- Try to **respond equally** to both poems.
- Prepare for the exam by completing **timed practice questions** so that you get used to including all your points in the time available.

# WRITING

**Question 1: The government is considering changing the law, so that parents will no longer be allowed to hit their children. Write a letter to the Prime Minister, where you *argue* the case that no one should be allowed to smack children.**

**B grade response**

Dear Prime Minister,

*Purpose and audience clear*

*Argument employs logic*

*Rhetorical question followed by strong 'And…' to develop the idea*

I know I am not alone in thinking that it is wrong to hit children. I cannot believe that any right-thinking person in the modern day finds such an action acceptable. If I am correct, then why has the government still failed to act on this matter? And that leads us to ask what you intend to do to improve the situation.

*Discourse marker 'of course', links to the other side of argument: dismissed in short last sentence*

Of course, some people you know will say that a slap does children no harm. They say it puts them on the right track and if given with love causes no damage. Yet that is just madness.

*'Punchy'/rhetorical question/paragraph*

We do not make murderers and rapists undergo corporal punishment, so why is it right to beat young children?

*Repetition in complex sentence to build to climax*

*Discourse marker 'What is more' introduces extra point*

Any parent who strikes a child is not showing love; any parent who strikes a child is teaching the child that violence is OK; and the parent who strikes the child is choosing to inflict pain rather than talk about the problem. It is easier to hit than to reason and a violent parent is a lazy one. What is more, their children are likely to turn out with those same faults and that same vilent attitude.

*Emotive image to win hearts and minds*

*Short sentences make strong, simple points: rhetorical exclamations*

We have all seen small boys and girls screaming in supermarkets and streets as their mothers strike them repeatedly to try to make them stop crying. It is the most ironic of situations. They cry more. Anyone would. Kids are in pain; and it is up to the government to save them.

*Audience addressed directly, still using emotive language*

*Firm conclusion*

You have a moral duty to prevent any further damage to those who can't defend themselfs. I hope you bring in a law soon that will end this suffering.

Yours sincerely,

Zoë Robinson

# EXAM PRACTICE: ANSWERS

## Some good points about this response

- The student makes the **purpose and audience clear** by addressing the Prime Minister directly in the greeting, and focusing on the title in the first topic sentence.
- The **strong and convincing style** is generally maintained throughout – aimed appropriately at the Prime Minister.
- It is **well structured**, with a clear introduction and conclusion.
- Paragraphs are varied and **support the argument**. For example, the short paragraph beginning 'We do not make...' makes a strong point clearly stand out from the rest.
- Sentences have a **wide range of appropriate lengths and constructions**. For example, the lengthy, complex list which uses repetition and semicolons effectively and opens the fourth paragraph, 'Any parent who...', can be contrasted with very short and direct sentences like 'Anyone would.'
- The **vocabulary is impressive** in places: 'ironic', 'undergo' and 'inflict', with discourse markers, 'of course', used effectively.

## How this response could be improved

- At times the style loses its formal tone, using 'kids' instead of 'children' and 'OK' instead of 'acceptable' or 'a solution'. **Greater consistency** would have created a better impression and possibly raised the grade.
- Better **linked and developed ideas** are needed at times, such as 'Kids are in pain', which needs more detail or better links with what has gone before.
- Although emotive language and rhetoric are used, the response might have benefited from **an anecdote, imagery or even appropriate humour** – perhaps sarcasm, e.g. 'I know you are probably doing your best but is it any good to anybody?'
- There are technical lapses. For example, 'vilent' and 'themselfs', and the rather confusing syntax in the sentence 'They say it puts them on the right track' i.e. who? A few minutes spent **checking for errors** would have helped.

## Don't forget...what you need to do when writing to argue

- Ensure you make the **purpose and audience clear** and keep them in mind when you write.
- Make sure your **arguments flow logically** – planning is essential.
- **Discourse markers**, such as 'because' and 'on the other hand', will help to develop your ideas smoothly.
- **Avoid conversational expressions and clichés** – credit is given for vocabulary that impresses.
- Sentences and paragraphs should be varied and not predictable. Using a **wide range of punctuation** will make the examiner respond positively to your skills.
- In argumentative writing, use **rhetoric, repetition and emotive language** to gain extra credit.
- Write as accurately as you can, avoiding any **careless errors** that will cost you marks.

# EXAM PRACTICE: ANSWERS

**Question 2: A recent report has shown that teenagers are less healthy than ever before.**
**Write an article for a school magazine, to *persuade* students to eat more healthily.**

*Addresses purpose in topic sentence*

*Examples to illustrate the point*

*Confident statement*

*Persuasive rhetoric – all of which is appropriate for the audience*

*Suggests there is a solution*

*Effective quotation*

*Re-emphasises points from previous paragraph*

*Structured answer to the problem – persuasive in its simplicity*

*Personal involvement*

*Humour to engage interest*

*List of benefits, again clearly intended to appeal to target audience*

*Appropriate conclusion*

### C grade response

Far too many students eat food that is bad for them. You only have to see what happens in the school canteen, as chips are downed by those who have school meals and crisps and sweets are eaten by almost everyone. It is time we put a stop to all this and think about our health and what is happening to our bodys.

Do you want to be overweight? Or would you like to wear a crop top without being embarrassed? Can you look at yourself in the mirror when you are going to bed? Do you keep wishing you hadn't had that chocolate bar – or those chocolate bars? Well, it doesn't have to be like that.

My mum keeps telling me, "All you have to do is eat a bit less and ~~exercise~~ exercise a bit more," and she's right. She knows that we all need to stop eating those burgers and fries and snacking all the time. I bet you do that, and it's time to stop.

For breakfast you could have some fruit and healthy cereal. That would make you much more alert for lessons. At lunchtime eat sandwiches and no crisps or try a salad from the canteen. I especialy like the cheesy ones. For dinner, ask your parents to give you something that fills you but doesn't make you fat. They won't mind that. They want you to be more healthy. In fact they'll probably be so pleased, they'll do a dance on the kitchen table and then give you a great big kiss – so I suggest you tell them when none of your friends are around!

Your new healthy way of eating will make you skin clearer, make you slimmer and get you that boyfriend or girlfriend you've been after. So it will all be worth it in the end.

# EXAM PRACTICE: ANSWERS

**The good points about this response**

- This is a grade C response because it consistently addresses **the purpose and audience**.
- It is **well structured** with an introduction, development and conclusion.
- A **range of punctuation**, (inverted commas, an exclamation mark and commas where appropriate), clarifies what is being said.
- It **engages the reader's interest** through its style, particularly through the use of rhetorical questions and humour.
- It **persuades from the beginning**, using examples, rhetoric, quotation, humour and a personal approach, rather than just writing about healthy eating.
- The student has **a point of view** which comes through strongly and allows for no doubts: 'It doesn't have to be like that', 'it's time to stop', 'it will all be worth it in the end'. Paragraphs often end with such statements, which is good because they stand out and help to persuade the reader.
- The ideas are linked together well, so that, although the student does not use discourse markers, it is **logical and the conclusion is convincing**.

**How this response could be improved**

- There is some **repetition of ideas** in the second and third paragraphs, which might be seen as effective but could be seen to show the line of thought has been temporarily stopped.
- Some **commas have been omitted**, for example 'In fact they'll probably...'
- The vocabulary is unambitious, e.g. '<u>eat a bit less</u> and exercise <u>a bit more</u>'. Examiners are looking for a **wider vocabulary**, which goes beyond what most people might use in casual conversation.
- Sentences are varied but usually **quite simple in construction**. There are few long sentences and more ambitious punctuation, such as colons or semicolons, is limited.
- One correction has been made, but other **careless errors remain**: 'make <u>you</u> skin clearer...', 'bodys'/'embarrased'/'especialy'.

**Don't forget...what you need to do when writing to persuade**

- Keep the purpose and audience in mind at all times. **Reread the title** regularly to ensure your writing is still focused on the task.
- **Be convincing**. In a persuasive piece of writing, you might not need to include an alternative viewpoint.
- Use the full range of your writing skills by **varying the paragraphing and punctuating consciously**, rather than relying solely on full stops and capital letters.
- **Use language imaginatively**. Don't write as you might to a friend but try to use more impressive words and phrases like the ones you might find in a newspaper article or a formal letter.
- **Engage the reader** by using rhetoric, quotations and examples.
- **Always check your writing carefully**. Presentation will only be an issue if the examiner cannot read what you have written, so do not be afraid to correct neatly.

**Question 3: People enjoy going to different places for interest and amusement. *Describe* a place that has made you feel happy.**

## D grade response

*Focus on a place*

In Blackpool the sun never seems to shine but we go there on holiday every year. There is wind and rain and my dad says he has to spend to much money on slot machines and my mum never takes enough warm clothes, but I still like it very much. I think its the best holiday resort, though I havent been to many others. It's a happy kind of place and I wish we could go there for two weeks instead of one.

*Clear images to interest the reader*

*Beginning to deal more obviously with the title*

*Anecdote brings the place to life*

Once i won a competition. You had to spot someone whose ear was printed in a newspaper and I found him on a peer. I had to go to a theatre that evening and we got free tickets and I was given £50 at the intervle. I think we spent alot of it on ice creams.

*Clear paragraphing throughout*

*Using vocabulary for effect*

The Tower makes me really happy when I see it. It sores up into the sky and you can see it from miles away, as well as the Pepsi Max. I love going on that every year, but I have never been up the tower because my dad says it's a waste of money.

*Description ranges appropriately to slightly different locations*

*Still relating to title*

We stay every year in the same bed and breakfast place with Mrs Smith. She doesn't stay with us she owns it. She still calls me Titch which i lothe. She is getting very old but we still think her house is wonderful! I especially love the breakfasts – they warm me up on cold mornings.

*Range of simple and complex sentences*

A good part of the holiday is going on the sands. If its sunny (a big if!) I sunbathe and usually some lads come round which is good because then I have people I can go round town with at night. My dad always says its dangerous, but my mum tells him its too cold for anyone to think about getting pregnant.

*Humour*

*Conclusion*

Anyway that's why I like Blackpool and I am always happy there. Well, nearly always.

## The good points about this response

- The student has **focused on the task**, describing a place that makes her happy.
- It provides the sort of information the examiner likes to see, such as **describing various elements of the resort and giving a quite personal view** through anecdotes, describing situations most people will recognise.
- The description includes **comments about the family** and their reactions, what happens in the resort, where they stay and how the young people behave.
- It uses some **humour**.
- It consistently **uses paragraphs**, even though they tend to be mechanical and deal with a particular subject without linking smoothly with what has gone before.
- There is a **range of punctuation**, moving beyond just full stops and capital letters, and a range of sentence types provide some extra interest.
- Some **vocabulary is used for effect**, for example 'sores up into the sky'.
- Some irregular words are **spelled correctly**.
- It comes to a definite **conclusion**.

## How this response could be improved

- So much **more could have been said**. The reader itches to know more about the place and why the writer is happy there.
- The **expression could be more effective**. At one moment, Mrs Smith seems to be one of the family, and the '(a big if)' is colloquial.
- More adventurous vocabulary could be used to create effects. In a descriptive piece especially, **similes and metaphors would add interest** for the reader.
- The **senses could have been used** to create the smells and sounds of the resort.
- In some ways, the whole description is **undermined by the final three words**, 'Well, nearly always' – which makes us wonder about the choice.
- **Punctuation needs to be checked** more carefully. Commas and apostrophes are sometimes omitted.
- The organisation is mechanical rather than flowing. **Paragraphs do not follow logically** from previous ones.
- There are **spelling mistakes and careless errors**, e.g. 'peer', 'intervle', 'alot' and 'i'.

## Don't forget...what you need to do when writing to persuade

- Organise your ideas so that you move logically from **an opening, through a development to a conclusion**.
- **Respond directly to the title**. Do not try to write a similar essay to one you have written before with a different title, purpose and audience.
- **Be imaginative**. You have studied poetry and fiction, and learned about the techniques used in imaginative writing. Now use these as models for your own writing.
- **Anecdotes, examples and precise descriptions** rather than generalisations are most likely to engage the interest of your reader – including the examiner.
- Technical accuracy is important. Avoid careless errors and, when you check through your work, **look out for sloppy expression and use of language**, as well as spelling and punctuation lapses.
- The wider the range of punctuation, the better. If you have the opportunity, show you can use **colons, semicolons, exclamation marks and can punctuate speech** correctly.

# EXAM PRACTICE: ANSWERS

**Question 4: Choose a sport, hobby or a way of passing the time that you enjoy. *Explain* why you enjoy it.**

### C grade response

*Simple but clear opening*

I love athletics. Some people say it's a strange way for a 16-year-old girl to spend her time, and even my friends think I'm a bit mad. When it's pouring with rain and dark and I'm doing a track session in February, I think I agree with them. But really it's my whole life and it gives me a real 'buzz'.

*Vivid impression engages interest*

*Begins to explain attraction*

I suppose what I enjoy most is running fast. It's great when I'm winning. There is a rush of adrenleen and if there is a crowd cheering it's even better. It makes all the hard work worth while.

*Explanation developed*

*Background to attraction*

*Emotive image*

It all started when I watched athletics during the Olympics years ago, I guess I was about seven or eight. I saw all the great runners and I wanted to stand on the presentation stand like them and get a gold medal and cry when the national anthem was played. Then I thought it would be great to win a race, be on television and be famous.

*Paragraphs linked/example used appropriate technical vocabulary*

*Effective complex sentence*

Now I watch Paula Radcliffe on TV and I hope that I will be as wonderful as her. So I train four nights a week, including endurance work, anaerobic sessions and some weight training and I even have a proper coach. When I was allowed to start with the wieghts I could hardly lift them at first because I'm very thin. A boy in the gym made fun of me and I screamed at him, but now he's my boyfriend and he helps me improve my lifting techniques, so I enjoy the gym work too.

*Moving to conclusion but still explaining*

Even if I never win an important really big race and become the best, I will still enjoy running and athletics. I have fun going away to competitions, it's great to be so fit. I think my friends are secretly jealous because I never put on any weight!

*Punctuation creates effect*

*Rhetorical flourish to finish*

Athletics is a sport for everyone, the people who take part in it are all friendly and it keeps you healthy and slim. What could be better?

# EXAM PRACTICE: ANSWERS

## The good points about this response

- A strength of this response is that **it explains throughout**.
- The writer gives the **feeling of really being involved** in what she has to say.
- It gives a **personal perspective**, particularly through the images – training in February, the boy in the gym – all of which help to sustain the reader's interest.
- **Paragraphing is clear and logical**. Each paragraph deals with a separate idea and there is some sensible linkage, 'Now I watch...'
- Sentences are suitably varied in terms of **length and construction**.
- There is some welcome **technical vocabulary**, such as 'endurance work, anaerobic sessions'.
- **Spelling** is mostly accurate.

## How this response could be improved

- Because of the way the topic is approached, 'I' features prominently as the subject in most sentences. **Greater variety of expression** would be more interesting, e.g. 'I suppose what I enjoy most is running fast' could become 'Running fast is an exhilarating experience'.
- Although there is a range of vocabulary, most is relatively simple and **could be improved**. For example, 'presentation stand' could become 'podium'.
- Care needs to be taken to **avoid repetition**, e.g. 'It would be great' and 'it's great' and 'the great runners'.
- Clichés, such as 'a sport for everyone', and conversational phrases, such as 'a bit mad', generally lower the tone of the writing and should be avoided.
- **The structure could be better**. For example, the paragraph beginning, 'Now I watch Paula...' links well with what has gone before but it is a weak topic sentence.
- New ideas are given in the final paragraph which could have been **explained and explored earlier**.
- There are some **spelling and punctuation mistakes**, for example, 'adrenleen' and 'wieghts', and the comma in the third paragraph should be a semicolon.

## Don't forget...what you need to do when writing to persuade

- **Respond to the title**, structure your answer clearly and move to an effective conclusion.
- Analyse through **examining details**, rather than just generalising about a topic.
- Impress the examiner by **varying sentences and paragraphs** and using a range of punctuation.
- Use vocabulary that is appropriate to the topic, including **technical vocabulary** when necessary.
- Explanation involves *why* something is done. Avoid just saying *what* happens – there must be a **detailed explanation**.
- Bring your response to life and **engage the interest of the reader** by using rhetoric, examples, imagery, quotation, anecdote, emotive language – and even humour.

# GLOSSARY

**adjective** a word that describes a noun: 'the tall cupboard', 'the round balloon'

**adverb** a word or phrase that tells you more about a verb: 'Chris whistled softly'

**advise** to offer information and suggestions about how someone should act or behave in a particular situation

**alliteration** the effect created when words next to, or close to, each other begin with the same letter or sound: 'several silent slithering snakes'

**analyse** to examine a text objectively, noting any significant features as to its structure, style, tone, use of imagery etc.

**annotate** to mark up with your own notes, which are usually made in the margin

**argue** to put forward a viewpoint

**atmosphere** the mood of a situation or setting.

**character** the personality of an individual in a fiction/non-fiction text, conveyed through their actions, words and thoughts, and through the actions, words and thoughts of others around them.

**chronological** the order in which a series of events occurred.

**clause** the building block of a sentence; each clause must contain a verb and normally includes a subject as well. Some sentences consist of a single clause: 'It was snowing.' Other sentences consist of two or more clauses: 'It was snowing and we were cold.'

**cliché** an over-used word or phrase, such as basically, to be honest, in any case.

**compare** to comment upon both similarities and differences between two or more texts/text types.

**complex sentence** a sentence containing one main clause and one or more subordinate clauses

**compound sentence** a sentence made up of two or more main clauses joined by a conjunction such as 'and' or 'but': 'Laura went skating but Judy stayed at home.'

**compound word** a word made up of two or more smaller words, such as schoolteacher, wetnosed.

**conjunction** a word that joins parts of sentences: 'and', 'but', 'if', 'although', 'as', 'where'.

**content** the ideas that the writer is trying to make clear to the reader (i.e. what the text is actually saying), not the methods the author uses to put these ideas across.

**evidence** information taken from the text to support your answer – see quotation

**fact** something that is known to be true and can be proved to be so; compare opinion.

**figurative language** the use of words or expressions in an abstract or imaginative way to create a particular impression or mood. Imagery such as metaphors, similes and personification are examples of figurative language.

**first person** a way of describing a text in which the writer or speaker refers to himself or herself by using the pronouns 'I' and 'we'; compare second person, third person

**form** the structure of a poem and the way it has been written – such as stanzas or free verse, rhyme patterns or rhythm.

**imagery** the use of language to create a vivid image or picture; metaphor, simile and personification are forms of imagery

**impersonal** writing that uses the third person ('he', 'she', 'it', 'they')

**influence** to try to affect the opinions/beliefs of the reader in more subtle ways than direct persuasion.

**inverted commas** punctuation marks used to show the beginning and end of direct speech ('Look out!' shouted Ali) or to highlight a particular word (the word 'genuine'). Also known as quotation marks.

**irony** a type of humour in which words are used to imply the opposite of what they normally mean

**metaphor** a form of imagery when one thing is said to be another: 'You are my sun and moon'

**mood** the 'feeling' created by the writer through words that reflect emotions and sensations.

**narrative voice** the 'person' that a writer uses to narrate a story: the two main narrative voices are first person (using 'I' and 'me') and third person (using 'he' and 'she')

**non-fiction** any form of text that is not fiction

**onomatopoeia** the effect created by words which copy the sounds associated with their meaning: 'crack', 'hiss'

**opinion** a belief or view about something or someone; compare fact

**organisation** the way in which the content is ordered to gain the reader's interest and understanding.

**paragraph** a section of a piece of writing, used to organise the argument or help readers follow the storyline. A new paragraph should mark a new topic or a change of focus; in dialogue, paragraphs mark a change of speaker.

# GLOSSARY

**personification** a form of imagery when an inanimate object is described in language that relates to animals or humans: 'The tree whispered'

**perspective** the point of view from which a text is written.

**presentation** the way in which a text is laid out on the page or on-screen.

**persuade** to try to convince a reader or listener to accept a point of view

**punctuation** a way of marking text with symbols (punctuation marks) to help readers' understanding. The most common punctuation marks are: apostrophe, bracket, colon, comma, dash, exclamation mark, full stop, hyphen, inverted comma (speech mark), question mark and semicolon.

**purpose** the function and intention of the writing.

**quotation** a piece of the text that you include in your answer (surrounded by 'inverted commas') as evidence to support your response.

**rhetorical question** a question that doesn't require an answer, used for dramatic or persuasive effect

**rhyme** a pattern that occurs when words or the endings of words share the same sound, especially in verse

**second person** a way of describing a text in which the writer or speaker refers to the reader or audience by using the pronoun 'you'; compare first person, third person

**sentence** a group of words that make sense. Sentences usually have a subject and a verb, begin with a capital letter and end with a full stop (or exclamation mark or question mark).

**setting** the place or environment in which a narrative/dialogue takes place – where it is set.

**simile** a form of imagery when one thing is compared to another: 'he had a face like a wrinkled prune'

**slang** familiar and very informal language, such as 'I've just about got used to…' or 'adults just don't get it…'

**structure** the way in which the writer uses devices such as paragraphs, headings and punctuation to make the content clear and easily understood.

**style** the method and approaches that a writer uses, for example through an imaginative choice of words, and use of literary devices such as figurative language.

**summarise** to pick out the main points of a text without copying from the passage or using quotations.

**symbolism** the way writers use words to suggest meaning beneath the surface, for example a cage may also symbolise a character's sense of imprisonment, a bird in flight, freedom, or a mist, confusion.

**techniques** approaches and methods used by writers to convey meaning.

**tension** suspense or uneasiness generated by a writer in order to add to mood and atmosphere.

**theme** the subject matter or topic of a fiction, non-fiction, dramatic or poetic text.

**third person** a way of describing a text in which the writer or speaker refers to somebody or something else ('he', 'she', 'it', 'they', 'Jessica'); compare first person; second person

**tone** the attitude and atmosphere that is communicated to the reader, created by the writer's vocabulary and sentence structure.

**verb** a 'doing' or 'being' word that describes an action, a happening, a process or a state

**viewpoint** an attitude or point of view.

**voice** the narrator or person speaking in a poem.

# INDEX

# INDEX

# Acknowledgements

The Publishers gratefully acknowledge the following for permission to reproduce copyright material. Whilst every effort has been made to trace the copyright holders, in cases where this has been unsuccessful or if any have inadvertently been overlooked, the Publishers will be pleased to make the necessary arrangements at the first opportunity.

'Remote, beautiful and pristine places such as Antarctica are having to 'work' increasingly hard to justify their wilderness status – so that one day they may be wildernesses no longer' by Jonathon Porritt, BBC Wildlife Magazine, March 2003, and 'The Maldives' by Mark Carwardine, BBC Wildlife Magazine, April 2003. Reprinted with the kind permission of BBC Wildlife Magazine and the authors

'Pay as you learn' by Christopher Middleton, from *Radio Times* 5th-11th April, 2003. Reprinted with permission of Radio Times

Extract from *Seize the Day* by Tanni Grey Thompson, published by Hodder & Stoughton. Reprinted with permission of Hodder & Stoughton Limited

Extract from '20 Dream Holidays for the 21st Century' by Jill Crawshaw, 26th January, 2003, in The Observer. Copyright © Jill Crawshaw. Used with permission

Extract from *Under Milk Wood* by Dylan Thomas, published by Dent. Reprinted by permission of David Higham Associates Limited

Extract from *Salt on the Snow* by Rukshana Smith, published by Bodley Head. Used by permission of the Random House Group Limited

From 'Limbo' by Kamau Brathwaite, from *The Arrivants: A New World Trilogy* published by OUP in 1973. Reprinted by permission of Oxford University Press

'Night of the Scorpion' by Nissim Ezekiel, from *Poverty Poems* published by OUP India. Reprinted by permission of OUP India, New Delhi

'Hurricane Hits England' by Grace Nichols, from *Sunrise* published by Virago in 1996. Copyright © Grace Nichols, 1996, both reprinted by permission of Curtis Brown Limited, London, on behalf of Grace Nichols

'This Room' by Imtiaz Dharker, from *I Speak for the Devil* published by Bloodaxe Books 2001, and 'Blessing' by Imtiaz Dharker, from Postcards from God published by Bloodaxe Books 1997. Reprinted by permission of the publisher, Bloodaxe Books

'Vultures' by Chinua Achebe, from *Beware Soul Brother* published in African Writers, Heinemann Educational, 1972.

'Presents from my Aunts in Pakistan' by Moniza Alvi, from *Carrying My Wife* published by Bloodaxe Books 2000. Reprinted by permission of the publisher, Bloodaxe Books

'Two Scavengers in A Truck, Two Beautiful People In A Mercedes' by Lawrence Ferlinghetti, from *These Are My Rivers*. Copyright © 1979 by Lawrence Ferlinghetti. Reprinted by permission of New Directions Publishing Corporation

'Not My Business' by Niyi Osundare, from *Songs of the Seasons* published by Heinemann Educational Books, Nigeria, 1990. Reprinted with the kind permission of the author

'Half-Caste' by John Agard, from *Get Back Pimple* published by Penguin Books 1996. Reprinted by permission of John Agard, c/o Caroline Sheldon Literary Agency

'Brother's plea to treat killer more humanely' by Lyndsey Rawie, in The Wakefield Express. Reprinted with the kind permission of The Wakefield Express

## Photographs
Charlotte Winn: p. 64
Corbis: p. 11
Oxford Scientific Films: p. 56
Popperfoto: p. 19,
REX Features: pp. 15, 43, 95
Science Photo Library: p. 23